MEMPHIS AND THE SUPER FLOOD OF 1937

MEMPHIS AND THE SUPER FLOOD OF 1937

HIGH WATER BLUES

PATRICK O'DANIEL

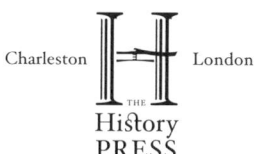

Charleston London

THE
History
PRESS

Published by The History Press
Charleston, SC 29403
www.historypress.net

Copyright © 2010 by Patrick O'Daniel
All rights reserved

Front and back cover images: *Courtesy of the Memphis and Shelby County Room, Memphis Public Library and Information Center.*

First published 2010

Manufactured in the United States

ISBN 978.1.59629.530.8

Library of Congress Cataloging-in-Publication Data

O'Daniel, Patrick.
Memphis and the superflood of 1937 : high water blues / Patrick O'Daniel.
p. cm.
Includes bibliographical references.
ISBN 978-1-59629-530-8
1. Floods--Tennessee--Memphis--History--20th century. 2. Memphis (Tenn.)--History--20th century. I. Title.
F444.M557O33 2010
976.8'053--dc22
2010026067

Notice: The information in this book is true and complete to the best of our knowledge. It is offered without guarantee on the part of the author or The History Press. The author and The History Press disclaim all liability in connection with the use of this book.

All rights reserved. No part of this book may be reproduced or transmitted in any form whatsoever without prior written permission from the publisher except in the case of brief quotations embodied in critical articles and reviews.

CONTENTS

Acknowledgements	7
Introduction	9
The City and the River	13
Setting the Stage	21
Return of the Machine	33
January Rain	43
High Water Blues	51
Flood Capital of the Nation	73
Superflood	85
Boss Rule	101
It's in the Bag	113
Epilogue	123
Notes	133
Index	151
About the Author	159

ACKNOWLEDGEMENTS

I received support and encouragement from a great number of people in writing this book. The staff of the History–Social Sciences Department of the Memphis Public Library and Information Center, whom I had the great pleasure to work with for so many years; they provided support, advice and access to many wonderful materials. I benefited from the input of all the staff, especially Dr. James R. Johnson, Wayne Dowdy, Gina Cordell and Sarah Frierson. Many people at the University of Memphis provided invaluable assistance, especially Charles W. Crawford, James Fickle and Frederick Knight, who served as my thesis committee, and Ed Frank and Christopher Ratliff who helped me in the use of the University of Memphis Special Collections. I want to thank Will McKay and the wonderful staff of The History Press for offering the opportunity to publish this work and Chris McCarthy of JenMar Communications, LLC, for technical support. A big thanks goes out to Sean, Rowan, Baba, Marcy, Frank, Margaret, Mac and Jeri for their encouragement. Most importantly, I could not have completed this work without the love and support of Kathy and Kelly, to whom I dedicate this book.

INTRODUCTION

Women and children were screamin' sayin' "Mama why must we go?"
Women and children were screamin' sayin' "Lord, where must we go?"
The floodwater have broke the levees and we ain't safe here no more.
      —*Lonnie Johnson,* Flood Water Blues, *1937*

The Webb family anxiously watched the water seep through the raised floorboards of their home. They had hoped that they could wait out this flood like the many others before and avoid having to abandon their Poinsett County farm and head for higher ground. The water reached six inches deep in the house and continued to rise when the Arkansans' hope gave way to terror at the realization the water would soon wash their home away. They had to act fast, so they braved the elements in the cold January night to escape while they still had a chance for survival.

W.A. Webb waded through the freezing water, hooked up the family's mules to their wagon and came back to the house for his wife and six children. They hurried into the wagon and quickly headed for the high ground of a highway near the town of Marked Tree. The husband drove the wagon as fast as possible, but their escape window quickly began to close as the yellowish-brown water from the overflowing St. Francis River swallowed their farm.

The family's worst fears began to come true as water rose over the wheels and the sides of the wagon. Their mules struggled to push through deepening water rising past their chests. The familiar terrain steadily melted away as the

Introduction

landscape morphed into a raging river. They had gone less than a quarter of a mile when the wagon wheels and the mules' hooves no longer touched the ground. Webb fought desperately to control the panicking animals as they swam through the torrent flowing over what had been a dirt road less than an hour before. The family sat waist deep in icy water, clinging to the wagon with only the mules' momentum keeping them from completely falling under the waves. They thought every minute would be their last until they finally saw the outline of the highway above the water in the distance.[1]

The Webbs traveled cold and wet to the nearby makeshift refugee camp. The overcrowded camp offered little protection against the elements, so they made their way south through flooded eastern Arkansas to the Harahan Bridge and crossed the raging Mississippi River to seek shelter in Memphis. Suspicious of the Red Cross and police, they avoided the refugee centers and took shelter in an abandoned two-room shack near the Memphis Municipal Airport shared by other refugees. Seventeen members of three families lived there together for weeks by surviving on minimal rations, struggling to stay warm and hoping to avoid forced internment in a crowded refugee camp.

Tens of thousands of desperate refugees rushed to Memphis fleeing floodwater in January and February of 1937. The mid-South frequently experienced flooding but not like this. This massive superflood broke all previous records, even those set in 1927. By mid-January it had devastated communities throughout the Ohio Valley, and then it moved into the rain-drenched Mississippi Valley. Overflowing tributaries paralyzed parts of west Tennessee and north Mississippi and turned much of the Arkansas delta into a small sea. As the Ohio floodwater washed across the mid-South, Memphians rushed to prepare for this new flood as they had in the past. However, as the full force of the flood came down on the surrounding areas, they soon found themselves dealing with a disaster on a scale never seen before.

The Ohio–Mississippi Valley Flood of 1937 proved especially challenging for Memphians. This new superflood broke all previous records set ten years earlier, sending nearly 60,000 refugees into a city of less than 350,000. Overwhelmed Memphians not only had to accommodate the survivors of this disaster but also had to save their city from a flood crest greater than any before in the United States. Press coverage of the events exposed the poverty of tenant farmers and the devastation of their homes and how Memphians rose to the occasion to aid them. The flood inspired impressive displays of charity and volunteerism, as well as deep prejudices and ulterior motives.

Historians have documented the superflood of 1937 and its impact on the country, but they have recorded little about the roles played by

Introduction

Memphians during this disaster, leaving gaps in our understanding of this important event. How did the local, state and federal governments work together in the mid-South? How did they care for the thousands of refugees? How did ordinary people participate in relief efforts? How did Memphians affect the outcome of the floods, and how did the outcome of the floods affect Memphians?

The author examines the parts played by Memphians during the Ohio–Mississippi Valley Flood of 1937 and its impact on the city. The work covers what roles the city and its citizens played in the disaster relief; how local political leaders responded to the flood; and what part Memphians played in flood control. It clarifies the importance of this city and allows for a better understanding of the local power structure and society of early twentieth century Memphis.

THE CITY AND THE RIVER

The flood was forty days in reaching its greatest height, which was the 20th of April, and it was a beautiful thing to look upon the sea where there had been fields, for on each side of the river the water extended over twenty leagues of land and all of this area was navigated by canoes, and nothing was seen but the tops of the tallest trees.
—Garcilaso de la Vega, chronicler of Hernando De Soto Expedition, 1543

Memphis overlooks the Mississippi River from the fourth Chickasaw Bluff at the crossroads of Tennessee, Mississippi and Arkansas. This piece of highland hosted Native Americans, Spanish soldiers, French traders, English explorers and the various military outposts and trading communities until the official founding of Memphis in 1819. Settlers had the convenience of access to the river and some of its tributaries while its elevation provided shelter against deadly flooding. River transportation allowed the city to grow from a small outpost to the focal point of an area made up of west Tennessee, north Mississippi, eastern Arkansas, southeastern Missouri and southwestern Kentucky, known as the mid-South. It also tied Memphis commercially with other river towns such as St. Louis; Cairo, Illinois; Vicksburg, Mississippi; and New Orleans. The river defines Memphis and its role in the region and the country. What happens to the river and what the river does to the surrounding area affects Memphis economically and socially. Memphis exists because of the river and, for better or worse, the fate of the river determines the fate of the city.

Memphis and the Superflood of 1937

The Mississippi River shapes the landscape through which it flows as well as the history and culture of the people along its shores. Its special mystique—an almost mythical quality—comes from its unique cultural and natural features. The river inspires stories, legends and music known worldwide. It evokes images of riverboats, cotton fields, epic Civil War battles, the haunting songs of Blues singers, the struggle for freedom and civil rights and, of course, broken levees and the rising tide of raging floodwater.

Spanish explorer Hernando De Soto named the river he found on May 18, 1541, Rio de Espiritu Santo, or River of the Holy Spirit. This vast river we now know as the Mississippi runs 2,340 miles from Lake Iasca in Minnesota to the Gulf of Mexico. It has the third-largest drainage basin, exceeded in size only by the watersheds of the Amazon and Congo Rivers. The basin covers more than 1,245,000 square miles, including all or parts of thirty-one of the United States and two Canadian provinces. It carries 41 percent of runoff in the United States to the Gulf of Mexico every year.

The Mississippi River also regularly floods neighboring low-lying lands, which, in turn, maintains numerous delicate ecosystems. Annual rains and melting snow cause rivers to overflow, clearing out natural debris and creating rich topsoil in the floodplains. Flooding also feeds the wetlands, nurturing many species of plant and animal life. It provides a habitat for millions of birds, as well as the occasional white-tailed deer, wild turkey, river otter, osprey or bald eagle. In addition, the river contains the most productive freshwater fish habitat in North America.

Settlers to the region found fertile floodplains for agriculture and a means of transportation for both people and products, which, in turn, fostered the growth of communities. These areas helped the growing population in many ways, but living near rivers also presented many problems. Unlike the native wildlife and vegetation, the new inhabitants did not mesh with the existing ecosystems. People soon began to attempt to force the rivers and floodplains to accommodate their needs. Tampering with the ecological structure of the landscape caused increased flooding, poor water quality, reduction of biological diversity and loss of wildlife habitat.

The wetlands played an important part in this structure because they slowed or held water back from the streams and rivers, thereby reducing the water's energy and ability to erode soil. It also stored water so that peak flows were reduced in wet times, and stream flows were maintained during dry times. There existed about forty-five million acres of wetlands in the Mississippi River watershed before the European colonization. By the twentieth century, only about nineteen million acres remained. Over time, settlers systematically drained much of the region's wetlands and put farms and towns in the floodplains, causing a breakdown of the natural buffer and an increase in the severity of seasonal flooding. Water that would have taken weeks or months to move downstream began to flow to the rivers in a matter of hours, resulting in more runoff than existing waterways could handle. The more land people urbanized or developed land for agriculture, the greater the flooding problem.[2]

Like most American cities, Memphis experienced population growth beginning in the late 1880s due to industrialization, improved transportation and expanding economy. However, Southern cities grew at a slower rate than their Northern counterparts. Birmingham and Atlanta lead the way in the South, while cities like Richmond, Nashville and Memphis only retained a leading economic position within their immediate areas. In its early days, large numbers of immigrants and settlers from the eastern United States inhabited Memphis, but the population began to change because of the yellow fever epidemics and the urban expansion at the end of the nineteenth century. A greater number of people moved to the city from the surrounding rural areas of Tennessee, Mississippi and Arkansas, and the children of early immigrants began to take on the characteristics of their new neighbors. These rural migrants brought with them their desire to create a better life as well as their attitudes and prejudices.[3]

Boosters made every effort to bring new businesses from the North to Memphis but they had to overcome long-standing stereotypes. They had to convince businessmen that their interests would remain profitable in a city known for crime, economic instability and lack of labor skills. Memphis at the beginning of the twentieth century had the largest urban population in the mid-South, though its character reflected the rural background of its inhabitants. The business elites who ran Memphis gladly retained the traditional values of the countryside but they also wanted to attract profitable new industry. This required recasting Memphis as a progressive, modern and business-friendly city. Pouring money into physical improvements and dealing with crime helped, but they still needed to show that Memphis had a capable workforce, efficient government and growing economy.[4]

Memphis entered a period of expansion following World War I with an emphasis on annexation and the attraction of new businesses. The economic prosperity—after the brief recession between 1920 and 1921—brought on by rebounding cotton prices boosted related industries such as cotton presses, warehousing and cottonseed oil plants. The city also became known as a distribution center for agricultural and steel products. It maintained its hold on the titles World's Largest Hardwood Market and the Hardwood Flooring Capital. E.L. Bruce Company began in 1921 and soon became the largest hardwood-flooring manufacturer in the world. By 1925, Memphis had over forty mills producing 300 million feet of hardwood lumber. Construction increased as seven new buildings went up in the downtown area and businesses opened in newly annexed parts of town. Plants for manufacturing furniture, hardwood flooring, boxes and automobile parts located in Memphis because of the nearby hardwood timber stands, the abundance of labor and the transportation services offered to distribute their products. The boosters of the Memphis Chamber of Commerce invited new Northern businesses to the city, including Fisher Body Works; a Ford assembly plant; Buckeye, Swift and Humko processing plants; and a Sears & Roebuck outlet. Cotton remained its lifeblood, but boosters hoped the new diversification would finally allow Memphis to compete economically with other cities.[5]

The city's business elites manipulated the image of Memphis to make it as attractive as possible to business investors. A series of annexations between 1899 and 1929 doubled the size of the city, and Harland Bartholomew's *A Comprehensive City Plan: Memphis, Tennessee* (1920) established an urban plan calling for construction projects that emphasized the downtown business district. Public works crews repaired and widened streets while new zoning ordinances set aside areas exclusively for industry. They eliminated the haphazard layout of the city while strict residential zoning kept the growing African American population in less visible areas of the inner city and near the northern and southern boundaries. However, expansion came at a price. The city grew beyond the Chickasaw Bluffs into low-lying areas susceptible to flooding, putting new businesses and Memphis's image at risk.[6]

The U.S. Army Corps of Engineers rigidly adhered to the flawed idea that levees alone could control flooding, even though all the scientific data about the river up to that time contradicted their assumptions. They understood that the current will accelerate when the quantity of water in a river increases, and a faster current scours the riverbed more than a slower current, deepening the river. However, the corps assumed that the levees-only method would promote such scouring to deepen the river enough to accommodate even the worst flood. To make matters worse, the corps opposed building spillways to let water out of the Mississippi River to ease pressure on levees and instead closed off natural reservoirs to maximize the amount of water in the river.[7]

Increasing flood levels began to take a toll on Memphis. In 1903, city officials placed a new levee system along the Gayoso Bayou, the waterway

High Water Blues

that ran through downtown Memphis. Engineers designed it to withstand a forty-one foot flood stage and included a pumping station to draw water from low areas and discharge it over the levee into the river. They had high hopes for the improved system, but the flood of 1912 exceeded the previous records and caused the levees to fail.

In the fall of 1912, the Tri-State Levee Association (later the Mississippi River Levee Association) formed and held a convention in Memphis to select delegates to attend the Rivers and Harbors Congress in Washington, D.C. They received additional money to repair levees damaged by the recent flood but, however, many collapsed again in the flood of 1913. After the levees failed again, the municipal government instituted a new plan to provide protection for a stage of fifty-two feet that included two huge intercepting tunnels to carry water to an improved pumping station on the Gayoso Bayou.[8]

After the 1912 and 1913 floods, Barnette Moses, a member of the Memphis Bar, wrote to the U.S. Senate, adding his voice to the chorus of those complaining about the corps of engineers' policies. He wrote that the floods had the same volume as the flood of 1882 but caused worse damage because of increased elevations of water resulting from the river's confinement. The river gauge at Memphis reached about thirty-six feet during the flood of 1882 but increased over the years to forty-five feet.

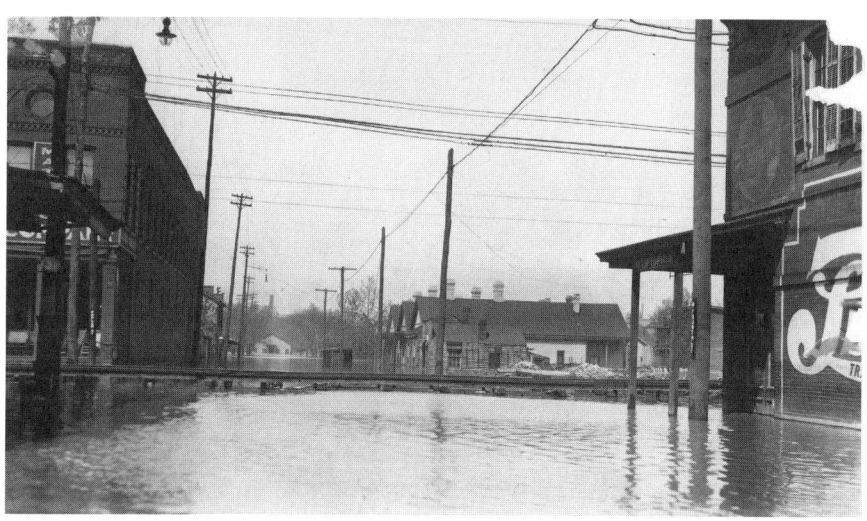

Fourth Street during 1913 flood. *Courtesy of the Memphis and Shelby County Room, Memphis Public Library and Information Center.*

Memphis and the Superflood of 1937

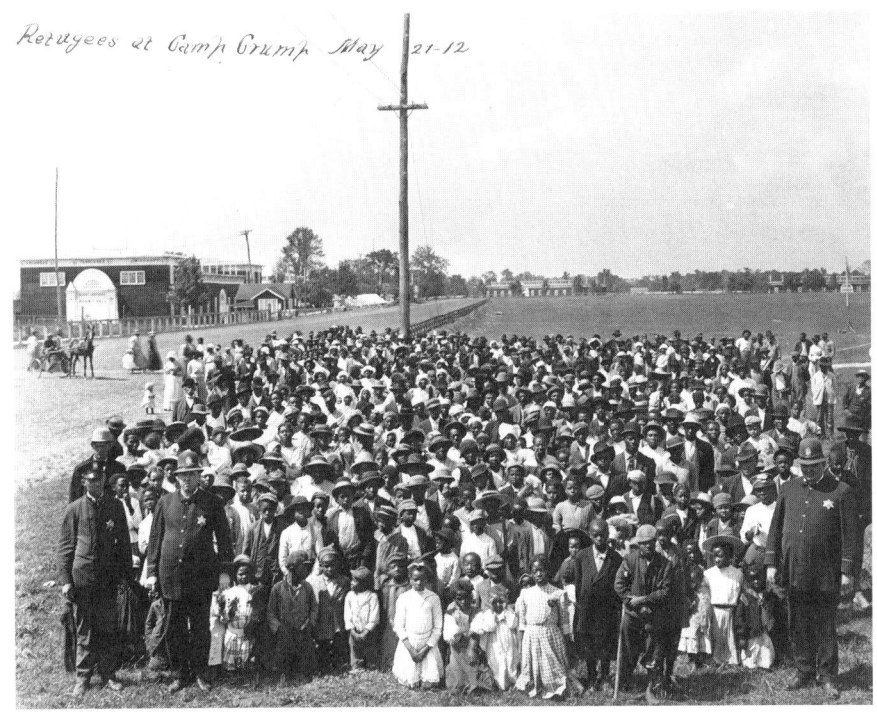

Refugees at the fairgrounds during the 1912 flood. *Courtesy of the Memphis and Shelby County Room, Memphis Public Library and Information Center.*

When the levees eventually gave way, the high water would rush into areas that were once safe from flooding. Just as Charles Ellet wrote sixty years earlier, Moses stated that flood control needed to include outlets, spillways and reservoirs to drain excess floodwater, thereby relieving pressure on the levees to prevent their collapse.[9]

In an address before the 1918 Southern Alluvial Land Association Conference in Memphis, local river expert Bolton Smith explained that flood control measures continued to fail because areas that acted as natural reservoirs were being blocked off by new levees. These reservoirs were needed to slow down the flow of floodwater and lower their levels. Smith's suggestions were mostly ignored. The idea of levees only persisted though it was clear that it was going to take more than levees to control the river.[10]

Lines of levees stretched along the Mississippi River by the twentieth century with no break or spillway in the entire thousand-mile line from Cairo, Illinois, to the Gulf of Mexico. However, regardless of how high engineers built the levees, the river would somehow find a way through.

High Water Blues

The Mississippi River Commission and the corps of engineers responded by building the levees even higher to a level based on the highest previous high-water mark. The more complete the system became, however, the more pressure the river exerted on the levees. Eventually, the ever-growing water levels exceeded what the levees could handle. In 1927, the spring floods exceeded all records, and when the levees gave way, so did the old levees-only policy. Another massive flood struck ten years later and helped cement a new approach to flood control. These events, centered largely in the mid-South, put Memphis at the center of two of the worst calamities in U.S. history that tested Memphians' resolve and brought to the surface their character as they played host to thousands of desperate refugees.

SETTING THE STAGE

When it thunders and lightnin' and when the wind begins to blow
When it thunders and lightnin' and the wind begins to blow
There's thousands of people ain't got no place to go.
—Backwater Blues, *Bessie Smith, 1927*

The massive Mississippi Valley Flood of 1927 made history not only as the worst flood to date in American history but also for its impact on the future of flood control and disaster management. It inundated approximately 27,000 square miles, ruined crops and damaged or destroyed over 130,000 buildings. The flood came in three waves, in January, February and again in April, keeping the affected areas underwater for most of the summer. Red Cross and the U.S. Weather Bureau estimated that the Mississippi Valley suffered between $250 and $350 million in flood damage. Memphis, at the center of the disaster, took on a prominent role in disaster relief that would lay the foundation for the part it would play in the next great superflood.

In August 1926, heavy rains drenched Nebraska, South Dakota, Kansas and Oklahoma before moving eastward into Iowa, Missouri, Illinois, Indiana, Kentucky and Ohio. Another low-pressure system heavy with moisture moving up the Mississippi Valley followed it, pouring precipitation over this same region. Two more storms followed the system and caused rain for weeks. On September 1, dozens of streams overflowed and flooded towns in a 350-mile area in the upper Mississippi. Another storm a few days later brought flooding to towns from Terre Haute, Indiana, to Jacksonville, Illinois, killing seven people.[11]

The rains continued over the rest of the Mississippi Valley through December. Nearly six inches of rain fell on Little Rock, Arkansas, in one day. In Tennessee, the Cumberland River flooded Nashville, and the Tennessee River flooded Chattanooga, killing at least 16 and making thousands homeless over Christmas. On New Year's Day, the Mississippi passed flood stage at Cairo, Illinois, staying above flood stage for the next 153 days. Rainfall resumed in mid-January and causing river levels to rise again, straining already weakening levees. At Memphis, the Mississippi River began rising on January 1, reaching a 37.8-foot stage on January 12. The water levels lowered to 20.9 feet on January 22 only to begin rising again. It reached 37.8 feet on February 12, never falling below 30 feet through the next month.[12]

The environmental damage caused by deforestation allowed water from the torrential rains to rush directly into streams and eventually the main channel, causing rivers' water levels to remain high all winter. Warm weather and early snow melts caused the upper basin to swell in the beginning of 1927, followed by more rain in the upper Midwest that sent full tributaries gushing into the already swollen Mississippi River. The floodwater poured down the Mississippi to the Gulf of Mexico with no break in the levee line. The flood crests flowed with such intensity that water backed up into the tributaries and, for a few days, the Ohio River actually flowed upstream.[13]

Snow fell from the Rockies to the Ozarks, and rain deluged areas in the lower Mississippi Valley in early March. The storms brought Mississippi four inches of rain on March 16. Three tornadoes touched down in the lower Mississippi Valley between March 17 and March 20, killing forty-five people and damaging levees. By the end of the month, every levee board south of Cairo had men patrolling levees twenty-four hours a day looking for breaches. Heavy rains prompted the weather service at Memphis to issue a warning to mid-South residents on March 21 that the river would probably reach a flood crest of forty-two feet. They warned owners of livestock and moveable property in low-lying areas to take appropriate actions.[14]

Memphis meteorologist Frederick W. Brist told reporters on April 12: "The future of the high water now depends on the movement of a storm centered today over northwest Texas. If it travels north we will miss further rain. If it goes over the Ohio Valley, there will be another tale to tell." Two days later, the storm system moved toward the Ohio Valley, bringing heavy

High Water Blues

rain to the St. Francis Valley areas from Cairo to Memphis and to the Cumberland River and breaking records set in 1913. The flood stage at Cairo reached fifty-five feet, breaking the previous record of 54.7 feet. Cairo meteorologist William E. Barron predicted the gauge would reach 55.5 feet by Sunday. The stage at Memphis rose $4/10$ of an inch in twenty-four hours to 42.3 feet, and the rush of floodwater threatened to break the record flood stage at Memphis of 46.6 feet.[15]

The situation took a turn for the worse on Good Friday, April 15, when six to fifteen inches of rain fell on an area from Missouri and Illinois, west into Texas, east almost to Alabama and south to the Gulf of Mexico. Delta counties in Mississippi received between six and fifteen inches of rain, while Greenville, Mississippi, received over eight inches. Forecasters at the national weather bureau announced that the flood from Cairo to the Gulf of Mexico "will be the greatest on record."[16]

The enormous amount of water overwhelmed levees along the main channel of the Mississippi River, causing nearly 200 levee breaks. The overflowing river covered 170 counties in Illinois, Missouri, Kentucky, Tennessee, Mississippi, Arkansas and Louisiana. The flooded area through the valley covered fifteen thousand square miles, an area larger than Belgium, three times the size of Connecticut and almost as large as Switzerland.[17]

The flood killed about 250 immediately, and deaths due to disease and exposure may have been over a thousand. The disaster displaced about 700,000 people. Floodwater inundated more than 26,000 square miles with depths reaching 30 feet; levees crevassed; and cities, towns and farms lay wasted. It destroyed crops, paralyzed industries and transportation and caused an estimated $1 billion in property damage at a time when the federal budget barely exceeded $3 billion.[18]

President Calvin Coolidge, who also served as president of the Red Cross, chose Memphis as the regional headquarters and supply depot and drafted secretary of commerce Herbert Hoover to run the overall operation. Hoover arrived in Memphis on the morning of April 25 with Major General Edwin Jadwin of the United States Army Corps of Engineers, Red Cross chairman James L. Feiser and Henry M. Baker, who oversaw distribution of supplies with the help of Red Cross financial representative Frank A Ellithorp. After a brief introduction to Mayor Rowlett Paine, the group posed for a picture for the newspaper and headed for the Peabody Hotel where they discussed the situation over breakfast. Hoover spoke to the press from the Red Cross headquarters in the Chamber of Commerce Building before inspecting the local refugee camp.[19]

Memphis and the Superflood of 1937

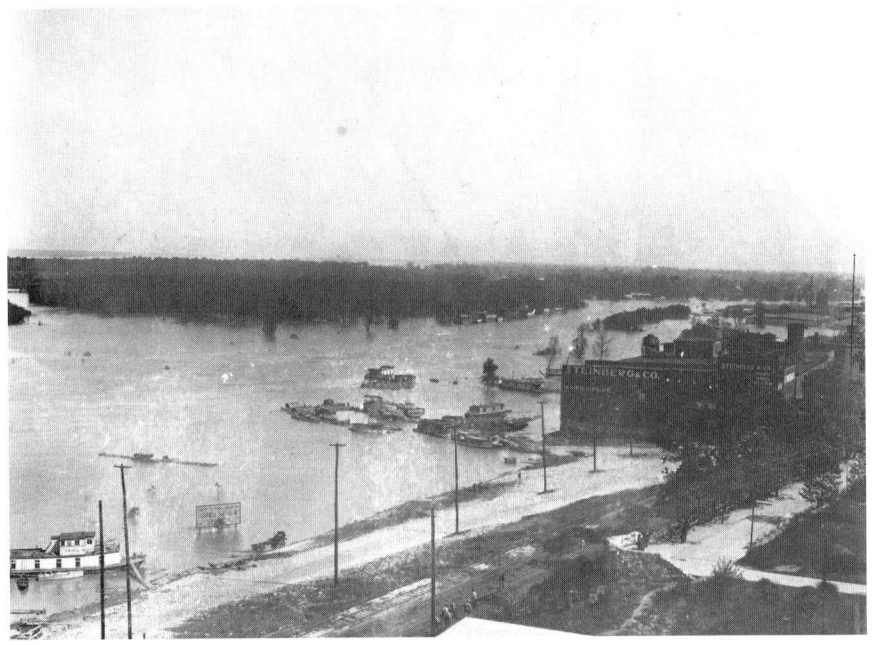

Memphis riverfront during the Mississippi Valley Flood of 1927. *Courtesy of the Memphis and Shelby County Room, Memphis Public Library and Information Center.*

Just as Mayor Edward Hull Crump had done during the floods of 1912 and 1913, Paine shut down the Tri-State Fairgrounds Amusement Park to the public and converted it into a facility for refugees escaping floodwater in eastern Arkansas, north Mississippi and west Tennessee. Police met arriving Arkansans at the Harahan Bridge and either escorted them or drove them by truck to the Red Cross camp where the mayor's emergency committee placed the occupants under armed guard out of fear of a rise in crime and outbreaks of disease.

By April 24, the fairgrounds held over one thousand flood victims. Once they arrived, the refugees received food, clothing and vaccinations against typhoid. The Red Cross then segregated them by race, placing white families in the automobile building and African American families in the stock building. Camp officials then sent male refugees to work on the levees. While men in good condition did levee work for $1.50 a day, women stayed to help maintain the camp by sweeping and mopping floors with antiseptics.[20]

Hoover made a nationwide appeal for donations from the WMC radio station. Coolidge refused to make federal money available, so relief efforts had to rely on money given by people around the country. Local volunteers raised thousands of dollars and collected food and clothing for the refugees. Theater owners put on benefit shows and landowners provided space for refugees' livestock.

Hoover, satisfied with efforts in Memphis, placed Henry Baker in charge of the Memphis headquarters with Colonel George Spalding supervising the growing fleet of rescue vessels and amphibious aircraft. Spalding soon had the distinction of commanding the largest inland water fleet in U.S. history. Boats made hundreds of trips into flooded areas with tons of supplies, often transporting refugees to Red Cross camps before returning to Memphis.

Rescuers made use of every available form of transportation and communication. Owners of commercial and private water vessels offered their services, and volunteers built additional johnboats. The U.S. Army and WMC set up satellite radio stations throughout the flooded areas in order to keep up with current conditions and relay requests for help, and the Interstate Commerce Commission authorized all railroads to disregard normal operations in favor of refugee transportation.[21]

On April 22, Dr. Louis Leroy, along with Thornton Newsum and Henry Colby, led a small flotilla of four motorboats with food, supplies and two hundred copies of the *Memphis Evening Appeal* to Greenville, Mississippi, following a massive levee break. Leroy had many accomplishments, including a career as a prominent pathologist, physician and a medical expert in legal proceedings. He installed Memphis's first X-ray machine, drove the first automobile in Tennessee and once played world chess champion Emanuel Lasker to a draw. Leroy also had an almost mythical reputation as a boat pilot and river-water sportsman, in part from providing immediate medical assistance to survivors rescued by Tom Lee when the *Norman* sank near Memphis in 1925.[22]

Leroy and his team of volunteers assisted in rescue and relief efforts in Mississippi and Arkansas with a "fleet of mercy speed boats." While in Greenville, they rescued at least two hundred people and established a hospital ferry to carry the sick to the King's Daughter's Hospital and hospitals for African Americans. Leroy helped medical authorities as well, assisting with the vaccinations of over four thousand refugees.[23]

The rescuers risked their lives many times during the two weeks spent in Mississippi. They faced many hazards, from crossing twisted railway lines and avoiding fallen wires. They could only cross railroads in low places, and they had to take care in passing under electrical cables. During one unfortunate incident, one of the crew had to have an arm amputated after he came in contact with a high-tension wire. Even their trip home presented dangers. They left Greenville on May 3, and three days later they had to avoid a tornado near Cat Island, which is opposite of Tunica Landing.[24]

One incident on the night of April 21 illustrates the dangers faced by those who worked on the Mississippi River during the flood. Eighteen workers waited aboard the government launch *Pelican* for transfer to the steamer *Wabash* at Knowlton's Point in Desha County, Arkansas. During the high winds, heavy rain and hail, the nearby levee suddenly broke and the river burst through the gap, carrying the *Pelican* along. The launch twisted, spun and sank within seconds. Only two of the crew survived. The rest, many of whom were Memphians, died when the launch smashed to pieces when it tumbled through the levee break. The staff of the Memphis newspaper the *Commercial Appeal* helped raise money for the widows and orphans of the lost crew.[25]

Aircrews faced danger as well. Storms forced down famed Memphis pilot Vernon Omlie while transporting vaccines to Little Rock. Others had to make emergency landings on tiny patches of land rising out of the flood. Red Cross supervisor Earl Kilpatrick died in an airplane crash after leaving Memphis on May 30.[26]

Hoover hoped to establish rehabilitation corporations to provide loans to farmers to rebuild once the floodwater subsided. However, the lack of enthusiasm from business communities disappointed Hoover. He made a special trip to Memphis at the end of May to address the Chamber of Commerce. He threatened to help African American workers leave plantations in Arkansas and Mississippi unless the group immediately raised $200,000. Members, many of whom owned plantations in question, agreed to meet Hoover's demand and raised the money within a week.

African Americans, who made up the bulk of the refugees, often faced abuse and civil rights violations in Red Cross camps that typified their plight in the South. Local law enforcement, national guardsmen and Red Cross workers kept refugees confined in order to ensure their return to their plantations and forced them into levee work details. The fairgrounds camp officials in Memphis kept refugees confined, but African Americans faired much better than their counterparts elsewhere in the Mississippi Valley. They had better food and the park commission provided entertainment, schools for the children and religious services.

In addition to accommodating refugees and providing relief, Memphians also had to protect their city from floodwater. Tributaries throughout the Mississippi Valley overflowed as floodwater backed up from the Mississippi

High Water Blues

River and Memphis's two tributaries, the Wolf River in the north and Nonconnah Creek in the south. The pumps at the mouth of Bayou Gayoso ran at nearly full capacity, pouring 1,300 cubic feet of water per second over the upper levee into the Wolf River. The business district in downtown Memphis rests on the highest part of the Chickasaw Bluffs, but the northern, southern and eastern parts of the city lie in lower areas more prone to flooding. By mid-April bayous swelled from rainfall and water from the overflowing Lick Creek covered parts of North Memphis around Vollintine Street and Tutwiler Street from Idlewild to McLean.[27]

Backwater forcing its way up the Wolf River and into bayous in North Memphis flooded three hundred homes in the Hollywood neighborhood, forcing evacuations for the first time since the flood of 1913. As the water continued to rise, a city engineer told reporters: "Absolutely nothing can be done to relieve the situation. We can only wait for the Mississippi River to go down." Residents of this largely African American neighborhood stacked belongings on homemade skiffs and waded through the water to higher ground. The Wolf River rose so high that it washed over the North Second Street Bridge. Morning rains on April 20 halted streetcars on the Hollywood line at Chelsea and Breedlove from 5:30 to 6:40 a.m.[28]

The river stage at Memphis reached 43.5 feet on April 16, and rainfall of 3.8 inches caused water to rise in already flooded areas in the city and county. Water covered the Hindman Ferry Road, Rugby Park Road and the Jones Avenue neighborhood and Paine Avenue near the Wolf River Sand Company. The overflowing Big Creek flooded Mount Vernon and Woodstock Road, and the Loosahatchie washed out Benjestown Road. The extensive flooding finally forced commissioners E.W. Hale and Luther F. Jones to close all highways in northern Shelby County.[29]

The South Memphis pumping station only had a limited effect on bringing the water levels down around the industrial area. City officials conscripted workhouse prisoners to reinforce the levees. Additional rain caused the Nonconnah Creek to rise a foot and a half higher than the Mississippi River, causing problems with roadways into Mississippi. A hump of sandbags held back floodwater from the point where Horn Lake Road intersected with the levee, slowing traffic. But the water did wash out a small bridge across Horn Lake Road that caused the closing of Florida Midwest Highway, one of the principal routes into Mississippi.[30]

Chief engineer William B. Fowler assured Memphians that pumping stations stood ready and the twelve-block-long levee from Auction to Bickford would hold against any flood stage up to fifty-two feet. Along the riverfront, workers added a foot and a half of sandbags to the levee protecting the Jones and Laughlin Steel Plant at the Navy Yard and bolstered the protective wall around the Illinois Central Railroad. Crews aided by a steam shovel worked through the night to reinforce the levee protecting industrial complexes while water lapped near the top of it. Navy Yard workers extended the protective wall from the foot of Jackson Avenue across the railroad tracks and raised the main levee in anticipation of the rising water.[31]

However, downtown and the riverfront still experienced problems. A cave-in at the foot of Illinois Street buried two small vacant houses. Firemen and police spent hours rescuing stranded motorists and homeowners who awoke to find water in their houses. As rains continued, lightning struck one of the pinnacles of St. Mary's Cathedral, tearing a hole in the roof that allowed water to damage the $10,000 organ.[32]

All traffic in and out of Memphis eventually resumed once the crest passed, allowing roads to reopen in Shelby County. Weaver Road and the Delta Highway–Lakeview Road opened again after two weeks, and crews removed sandbags that held back water from Horn Lake Road. However, Memphis still felt the effects of the flood well into May. An overflowing bayou caused flooding on Jefferson Avenue from the Memphis Steam laundry to North Pauline Street. Numerous other streets flooded as well, and homes in these areas lost telephone service.[33]

Memphians had to deal with considerable flood damage, but not as much as other communities throughout the Mississippi Valley. Paducah, Kentucky; New Madrid, Missouri; Clarendon, Arkansas; and Greenville, Mississippi, suffered devastating losses. Memphis, because of its location on the Chickasaw Bluffs, avoided the worst of the flood. Its location not only provided protection but allowed the city to play a vital role in Red Cross relief operations, which added to the prestige of the city. The actions taken during the 1927 flood provided city officials and the Red Cross with a blueprint for dealing with future disasters.

The Red Cross headquarters in Memphis certainly lived up to Hoover's expectations. It linked federal, state and quasi-governmental entities and private citizens and businesses into a surprisingly smooth-running administrative machine with streams of coordinated responses, known as field operations letters, delivered by telephone, radio and messenger.

Hoover stated:

> *At Memphis we have coordinated under the Red Cross, not only the personnel, equipment, and supplies of the federal departments, but also*

> *coordinated with local citizens, committees, Red Cross chapters, state officials, departments of health, national guard, American Legion, and others engaged in the common problem. The organization comprises shelter, food supply, medical supply, boat control, railway transportation, accounting, and other necessary working divisions. Due to the fine devotion and spirit of all these organizations, it is possible to say that there is practically none in the territory behind the flood crest who is not now receiving sufficient food, shelter, and medical attention. The states are preserving order and have taken vigorous measures to maintain public health. There is suffering incident to the flood, but it has been minimized in every way humanly possible.*[34]

In the aftermath of the 1927 flood, politicians and engineers argued for months over the issue of improving flood control. Many of the old guard, including Coolidge, Jadwin and Hoover supported the old method of relying on levees only to control flooding. However, the public's lack of confidence because of the large number of levee breaks left an opening for those who hoped to utilize other methods. The two sides eventually reached a compromise after months of debates, resulting in the Flood Control Act of 1928, later known as the Mississippi River and Tributaries Project. On May 15, 1928, President Coolidge signed the act into law that committed the federal government to a definite program of flood control, including new levees, as well as floodways, channel improvements and stabilization and tributary basin improvements.

While the United States Congress debated over flood control legislation, those in the Mississippi Valley worried about the next superflood. Southerners awaited the next wave of high water from melting northern snow and seasonal rain. Memphis had much less physical damage than other communities throughout the Mississippi Valley; however, the 1927 flood caused concerns about the trend of worsening floods and the city's increased vulnerability. In addition, its economy—so closely tied to transportation and distribution—suffered because of the flood. Memphians welcomed the new flood control measures in hopes that they would keep the city secure from future superfloods and protect their investments in surrounding areas.[35]

The 1927 flood broke down the old ways of thinking about flooding, causing significant changes in policy and technology both on the national and local levels. Governing bodies including the U.S. Army Corps of Engineers and local governments had to rethink their approaches to flood-control technology and disaster management as they came to terms with what appeared to be a new trend of catastrophic flooding. The enormity of the 1927 flood not only opened people's minds to the possibility of future superfloods, but it also left them with a sense of anxiety over how to deal with them. Engineers finished most of their work on the main channel of the Mississippi River over the next ten years, but the tributaries still needed work.

A flood struck west Tennessee and north Mississippi in January 1935 and, like an ominous warning, it gave mid-southerners a taste of what awaited. Like a miniature tidal wave, floodwater from a levee break at Marks, Mississippi, on the Coldwater River covered an area forty miles by fifteen to thirty miles and drove thousands from their homes. Bitter, freezing cold brought misery piled on misery for locals and caked the flood's backwash with a two-inch crust of ice. Hundreds of shivering refugees trudged into the towns of Sledge, Dundee, Sarah and Savage. Volunteers in motorboats rushed in to pluck shouting and praying flood victims off rooftops and out of trees. The same rains that swelled the Coldwater River flooded nearby streams in Tennessee and Arkansas. By the end of the week, floodwater marooned an estimated twenty-five thousand mid-southerners and killed another twenty-seven.[36]

Seven inches of rain fell on Memphis in three days, causing damage in the low-lying areas around the northern and southern parts of the city. The normally sluggish Wolf River became a torrent, washing out the North Second Street Bridge and flooding Highway 51. Three feet of water covered areas around Highway 78 (Lamar Avenue) and Brooks Road.[37]

A second flood struck the mid-South in March, once again overpowering levees along the tributaries of the Mississippi River. Floodwater in eastern Arkansas broke through levees in eighteen places along the St. Francis River and thirty-four places along the White River. Frightened farmers overpowered guards and dynamited levees to save their farms along the Tallahatchie River in north Mississippi. Shelby County sustained an additional $444,000 in property damage, although Memphis had relatively minor damage because of recent revetment work and the construction of Riverside Drive.[38]

Areas farther up the Ohio River suffered much worse damage. New England and the Ohio Valley had an unusual amount of flooding beginning in March 1936, causing extensive damage. In addition, it kept soil saturated and caused waterways to remain unusually high. By January 1937, these areas could not absorb additional rainfall and were in no condition to receive more rain.

High Water Blues

Mid-southerners remained uneasy about the state of flood protection following the floods of 1935 and 1936. Even though the Mississippi River and Tributaries Project addressed the issues of large-scale flood control, a great deal of uncertainty remained about its effectiveness, especially along the tributaries. With the new flood control measures remaining not fully tested and work still needed, one question remained: was it enough to protect the Mississippi Valley from the next superflood?

RETURN OF THE MACHINE

For Memphis has a totalitarian government...similar in character...to that of Mussolini and Hitler, though so far [its people are] *not disturbed enough to rebel or even form an underground.*
—*Anonymous criticism of Memphis,* Economist *(London), 1943*[39]

Edward Hull Crump headed the local political machine that ran Memphis and influenced state politics in the first half of the twentieth century. His single-minded vision of the municipal efficiency drove him to become the most powerful figure in the city's history. Many praised his efforts while others balked at his strong-arm tactics.

A cynical reporter wrote:

> *Ed Crump holds no public or political office, but his Shelby County Democratic Organization is probably the smoothest, most efficient political mechanism in the U.S. In his thirty-seven years of benign if iron despotism, he has given Memphis citizens almost everything but the right to vote for a candidate of their own choosing—a luxury he firmly believes that few but the maladjusted miss anyhow.*[40]

Crump was born forty-five miles south of Memphis near Holly Springs, Mississippi, in 1874. After his father, a former Confederate officer, died in 1878 from yellow fever, his mother moved the family to Holly Springs. There he completed his education and took a number of lackluster bookkeeping

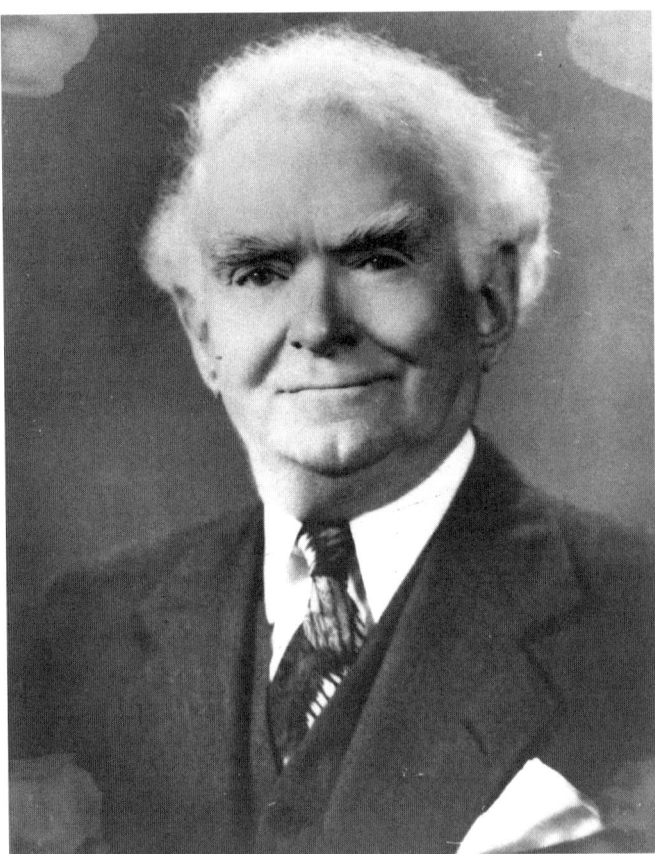

Edward Hull Crump, the most powerful man in Memphis. *Courtesy of the Memphis and Shelby County Room, Memphis Public Library and Information Center.*

jobs. Unsatisfied with his career prospects, Crump, like many other mid-southerners, moved to Memphis with hopes of better opportunities.[41]

As the story goes, nineteen-year-old Crump arrived in Memphis with only twenty-five cents in his pocket. He worked his way up in a saddle and carriage firm and, most importantly, he married well. His marriage to Bessie Byrd McLean allowed Crump into the upper echelons of Memphis society. The subsequent business opportunities, including the establishment of the city's leading insurance firm, made him a millionaire. It also gave him access to politics at a time when the upper classes felt the pull of progressivism. Crump cast himself as the champion of honest and efficient government. He promised to reform the corrupt and wasteful city government, improve the fire and police department, repair the swampy streets and improve garbage collection. The reform campaign won over voters and allowed Crump and his supporters to replace the Walsh–Malone machine with their own. Crump served on the Board of Police and Fire Commissioners beginning in 1907, led the drive to establish a commission form of government and was elected mayor in 1909.[42]

Crump's administrative ability allowed him to build a loyal political machine and run an efficient, but corrupt, city government built on favoritism. His political success came without making a single political speech. Instead, he allowed others to make speeches on the main streets and negotiate on the back streets with the six hundred saloonkeepers and ward bosses for their support. He waged a brief publicity war on vice but then permitted the underworld to run free. Crump made use of protection money paid by illegal gambling, prostitution and alcohol interests and poll taxes to control elections.[43]

Crump established a template for future relief operations in Memphis during the floods of 1912 and 1913. Each time, he oversaw the care of nearly two thousand Arkansas refugees who fled floodwater for sanctuary in Memphis. Crump formed a relief committee headed by R.O. Johnson. James P. Krenz, secretary of the Memphis Relief Committee, served as relief committee secretary and raised about $18,000 for relief. The city cared for the flood victims but, at the same time, kept them at a distance by confining them to a makeshift refugee center at the Tri-State fairgrounds. The state militia maintained the facility—renamed for the occasion as Camp Crump—and local volunteers helped care for over seven thousand head of livestock belonging to the displaced flood victims. Memphis mounted police provided security and one officer volunteered as head cook. The federal government supplied daily rations while the Metropolitan Life Insurance Company provided milk for the nearly three hundred babies. The refugees did the manual work around the camp "under the direction of departmental superintendents."[44]

The city's nursing service, organized by Crump in 1910, provided medical assistance for both white and black patients. Memphis hospitals set aside beds for the seriously ill, mostly sick with pneumonia, while the board of health supplied a sanitary squad for the camp. Board members closely monitored the camp's cleanliness and the state of the refugees' health for any signs of contagious disease. On one occasion, a case of spinal meningitis prompted the nurses to start "spraying throats" to prevent more outbreaks.[45]

Crump consolidated a power base through favoritism and vote manipulation that allowed him to win elections in 1911 and 1915. He used his position to create a political machine partly financed by vice interests, protection rackets and alcohol dealers who operated openly in violation of the state prohibition law. The machine proved powerful but not invulnerable to its opponents. Newspaper editor C.P.J. Mooney, attorney Guston Fitzhugh and local "church folk" led the attack on Crump's involvement with liquor interests. Fitzhugh introduced an ouster petition against the mayor based on the Elkins Act of 1915 that provided for the removal of state, county or municipal officials who failed to perform their sworn duties, who were publicly intoxicated, who engaged in gambling or who violated a penal statute of moral turpitude. All courts had jurisdiction, and any defendant found negligent could be removed from office. Crump's enemies took advantage of this and accused him of not enforcing the Nuisance and Anti-Shipment Acts of 1913 that outlawed houses of prostitution and gambling and the transportation of liquor.[46]

Crump admitted the charge, and the lower court ordered his removal with the state supreme court upholding the decision. The move worked but it only affected the old term; Crump won the next election, and his term was to begin January 1, 1916. Fitzhugh promised to reintroduce the suit along with further charges of corruption. Realizing he was about to be run out of office, Crump followed the only reasonable course of action: on February 22 he took the oath of office, collected his back pay and resigned as mayor. However, he never admitted guilt. Instead, he cast himself as a victim of evil private power corporations who had conspired against him out of fear for his plan to create public power corporations. Crump focused on insurance and Coca-Cola franchising while waiting for his chance to take the reins of Memphis once again.[47]

Crump still had significant influence in local politics despite the fact the courts denied him the mayor's office. Crump took office as Shelby County trustee six months after his departure as mayor, and through his position he maintained much of his network of handpicked politicians and close alliance with Senator Kenneth Douglas McKellar. Even so, he needed to gain access to the mayor's office. At the last minute he threw his support behind Mayor Rowlett Paine's reelection campaign against a Ku Klux Klan candidate, allowing him to win by a small majority in 1923. The favor should have bought Crump more influence with Paine, but the mayor remained just out of Crump's complete control. Crump realized he needed to handpick someone for the mayor's office who was more inclined to do his bidding.

Herbert Hoover and Huey Long capitalized on their performances during the flood to help win elections. However, Paine never got the chance despite an impressive showing at Mayor William Hale Thompson's national flood control conference in Chicago in June 1927. His participation in Thompson's conference instead left him unprepared for an attack by political opponents.

Crump's aspirations to control Memphis again put him on a collision course with Paine, and the mayor soon found himself outgunned by the determined political boss. Crump looked for a chink in Paine's armor and found it with a bootlegger named John Belomini. Federal agents raided Belomini's store and found a ledger containing an apparent list of bribes paid to local police officers. Paine, occupied with the Chicago flood control conference, did not find out from investigators but rather from a newspaper reporter after he returned to Memphis. Embarrassed, Paine asked federal authorities to launch an investigation of the police department rather than Attorney General Tyler McLain, a Crump supporter. When federal judge Harry Anderson refused, saying the case fell within local jurisdiction, McLain used the incident to discredit Paine.[48]

McLain threatened to remove Paine and Police Commissioner Thomas Allen unless they proceeded with an investigation. The report by the City Club, a local civic organization, on July 30 further embarrassed Paine by stating that the mayor was wrong to not let the club initially examine the ledger and the police department was riddled with corruption. Commissioner Allen suspended forty-one police officers after a board charged them with inefficiency, incompetency and conduct unbecoming an officer. Crump supporters found evidence that the officers actually received suspensions because they refused to support Paine's reelection. Attorney Charles Bryan pointed out the lack of proof that any of the officers ever received any payoffs at all, and the trial board eventually declared the officers not guilty.[49]

Meanwhile, Crump courted defecting middle-class progressives along with disgruntled African Americans. In 1923, Paine guaranteed new streetlights, street paving, a new high school and the appointment of black firemen and police officers. Reneging on his campaign promises as mayor cost the support of this powerful voting block. In 1927, Robert (Bob) Church Jr, Wayman Wilkerson, George W. Lee and Dr. J.B. Martin established the West Tennessee Civic and Political League to oppose him.[50] Hoping to use fear to win back white voters, the desperate Paine claimed that his opposition's victory would guarantee black political ascendancy. He accused Crump of trying to rule through proxy and the election of his opponent Watkins Overton would mean an end to white control of Memphis; few listened. Crump's handpicked candidate won the election and ushered in a new era of machine rule.[51]

In the beginning Overton had two qualities that appealed to Crump: his air of respectability and his loyalty. His grandfather John Overton Jr. served as mayor from 1881 to 1883, and his great-grandfather Colonel John Overton

MEMPHIS AND THE SUPERFLOOD OF 1937

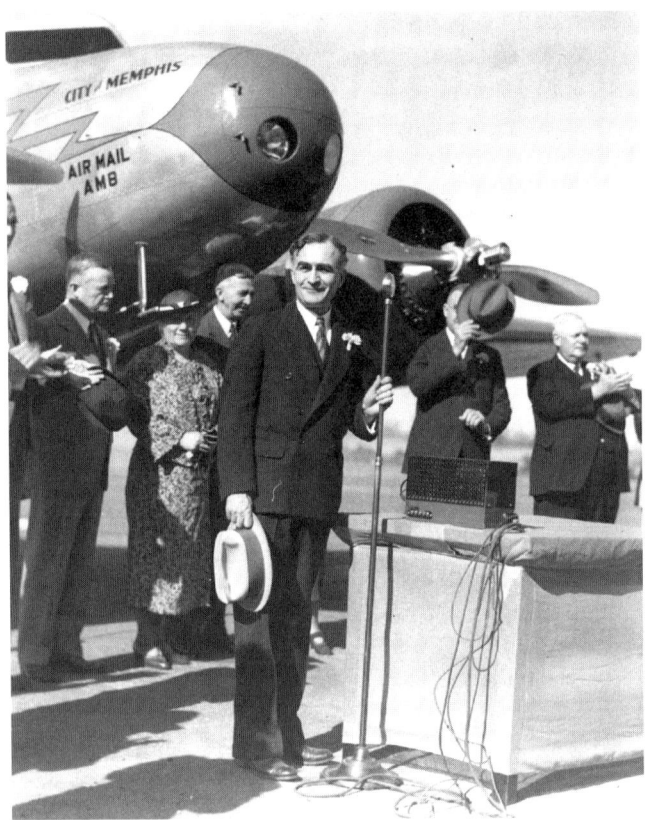

Watkins Overton, Boss Crump's hand-picked successor to Mayor Paine. *Courtesy of the Memphis and Shelby County Room, Memphis Public Library and Information Center.*

helped found the city. Overton had a bachelor's degree from Harvard and a law degree from the University of Chicago. He served on the Tennessee state legislature in 1925 and went to the state senate in 1927. There he caught the eye of Crump who selected him to run for mayor. At thirty-four, Overton became known as the Boy Mayor of Memphis, even though he was only a year younger than Crump when he first became mayor. In fact, Overton ran virtually unopposed for twelve years. Crump said "Overton will be the absolute mayor of Memphis without dictation or embarrassment from me." However, most understood the true nature of their relationship; Memphians knew Crump intended the new mayor to act as an extension of his power.[52]

Crump men held key positions that maintained the machine's network. Crump's right-hand man Frank Rice managed all Crump's campaigns, enforced discipline and oversaw the registration and voting of African Americans. He also served as Crump's liaison with the Shelby County Democratic delegation at the state legislature in Nashville. Although Rice only served once as an elected member of the legislature, he directed the Memphis legislators who voted as a block according to Crump's wishes. Commissioner E. William Hale governed Shelby County; Oscar P. Williams headed the carpenters' union and commissioner of public works; and Will Gerber served as city attorney. Most importantly, city engineer William Bingham Fowler and Congressman Walter Chandler held key positions that allowed them to carry out Crump's wishes to ultimately restructure the city's flood-control system.[53]

Fowler began his career as a water boy for city engineers in the sewers in 1900. He attended the Naval Academy in Annapolis, Maryland, but did not complete the program. He returned to Memphis and worked his way through the ranks of the city engineer's office, acquiring his engineering skills on the job. He left to work as the park superintendent and run a short-lived construction company. He returned to the city engineer's office in 1918 and became chief engineer only nine months later. He later supervised many important projects through the 1960s including President's Island, Crump Stadium, the construction of over four hundred miles of sewers and the routes of the interstate highways around Memphis as well as flood-control measures for the city.[54]

Walter "Clift" Chandler played an important role in Memphis politics and Crump's political machine as well. Born in Jackson, Tennessee, on October 5, 1887, he attended public schools before going on to earn his law degree at the University of Tennessee in 1909. He was admitted to the bar the same year and began practice in Memphis. He entered politics in 1916, becoming the assistant district attorney general and member of the state house of representatives the following year. He left the House to serve as a captain in the 140th Field Artillery, 13th Division, American Expeditionary Forces, from July 25, 1917, to April 19, 1919. After his return, he served in the state senate from 1921 to 1923, as city attorney of Memphis from 1928 to 1934 and represented Tennessee's Ninth Congressional District beginning in 1935 until his resignation in 1940 after winning his first mayoral election in Memphis. He served as mayor again in 1943 and 1953 and filled an unexpired term in 1955. He also taught school, reported for the *Knoxville Sentinel*, served as temporary president of the Tennessee constitutional convention and authored the federal Chapter 13 bankruptcy legislation in 1937.[55]

Aside from controlling key local politicians and their subordinates, the machine had the ear of the Republican president. Two weeks after the 1927 August primary, President Herbert Hoover invited Overton to meet with him at the White House. Overton's suggestion that increased flood-control projects on the Mississippi River could help alleviate unemployment in Memphis interested Hoover. The president reacted favorably to his request, doubling the appropriation to $70 million. Hoover still had a great deal of interest in the Mississippi Valley and strongly supported flood-control measures, even though his actions strengthened the Democratic machine's political position. Successfully negotiating for additional relief funds gave the appearance the machine was "powerful enough to squeeze federal funds from a tight-fisted, recalcitrant president like Herbert Hoover."[56]

Not everyone benefited from the expansion of the Crump Machine. The events at the beginning of 1937 illustrate the difficult position of African Americans within the legal system, politics and residential structure of Memphis. While no African American ever entered the inner circle of the organization, some acquired political leverage because of the importance in securing votes during the ascendancy of the Crump Machine. In one case, Robert (Bob) Church Jr. organized thousands of black voters for Mayor Overton's candidacy in 1927 and, in return, the machine granted occasional favors. However, the importance of the African American vote diminished as the machine became more entrenched in the 1930s. The occasional cooperation between the Republican Church and staunch Democrat Crump became less frequent because of Church's waning influence following the elections of the new Democratic president.[57]

Black Memphians collectively held more power than most African Americans in the South but they still lacked the same rights or privileges as whites and continued to suffer from frequent violations of civil liberties and police brutality. For example, incarcerated African Americans were often used as forced labor on plantations. Beginning in the 1920s, the courts encouraged African American inmates to work off their fees in cotton fields in eastern Arkansas in lieu of jail terms. Even the machine-controlled Works Progress Administration programs often routed black workers into the same fields despite objections from the African American community.[58]

African Americans existed not only socially on the fringe but physically as well. Blacks played an important part of the workforce, and their votes proved useful during elections, but, for the most part, city planners made every effort to keep them out of sight. Zoning laws forced them to live in some of the worst parts of the city, including areas near swamps, creeks and bayous, where flooding and disease were most frequent.[59] All of these factors contributed to the excessive hardships suffered by African Americans during the Depression and especially the 1937 flood.

High Water Blues

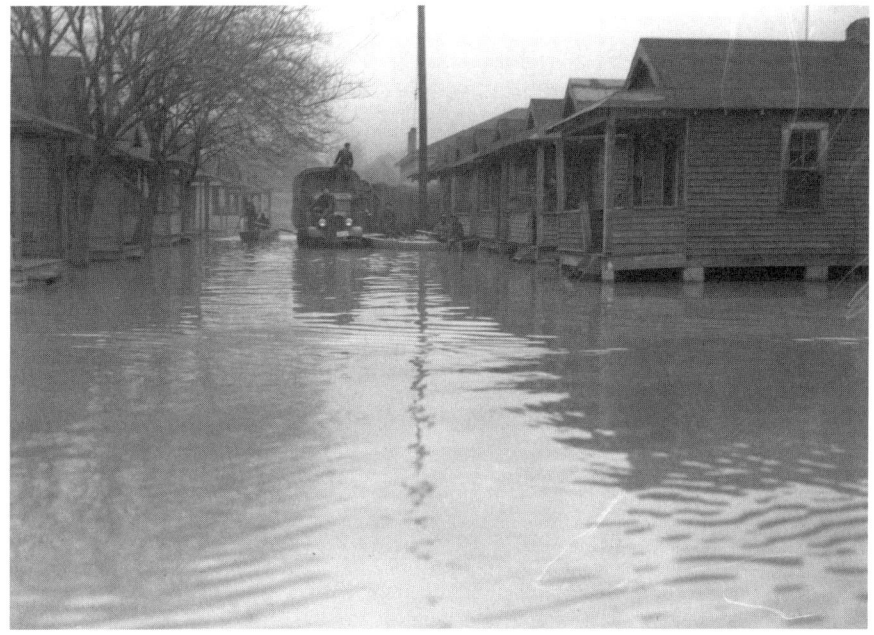

Flooding in a North Memphis neighborhood in 1937. *Courtesy of the Memphis and Shelby County Room, Memphis Public Library and Information Center.*

Expansion of the city meant greater power for the political machine. By the 1920s, progress became the catchword of the day as city planners expanded the city limits far beyond the high ground of the Chickasaw Bluffs. The city steadily annexed areas for new industry attracted by city boosters and to accommodate the desire of the wealthy for a suburban fringe beyond the poverty of the zone of emergence. Meanwhile, key government officials accumulated a new range of power as they doled out jobs to the faithful to cover the extension of old and new city services into newly annexed areas.

Improvements in transportation and roads facilitated the industrialization of northern and southern extremes of the city, but planners paid a price: these newly developed features fell in areas subject to flooding. Allowing the new Ford plant near the Nonconnah Creek or the Firestone plant near the Wolf River to be damaged would have hurt the city's chances of attracting future businesses. This was not a sacrifice Crump would allow happen.

Crump maintained his position of power with a careful balancing act: He had to appease both whites and blacks in order to secure votes and create a stable environment in the city. As a member of the U.S. House of Representatives from 1930 to 1934, he had to balance the interests of the local business elites with those of his most important benefactor, the president, and he had to continually prove to his adversaries as well as his followers that he fully controlled the city.

The first few months of 1937 tested the machine's worthiness to rule Memphis. Even though the challenge came from nature rather than some clever politician or righteous attorney, failure would have had serious consequences. Damage from floodwater and groups of disorderly refugees would have injured Memphis's carefully honed image of a clean, safe and progressive city. It would have impaired the machine's ability to attract new businesses, expand city services and generate jobs. What was at stake was not simply the fate of lives and property but the machine's reputation as an effective political organization.

JANUARY RAIN

The movement of floodwaters is an example of the blind legality; one might almost say the constitutionality of nature. There is no appeal from it and no amending process.
—Robert Luther Duffus, the New York Times, *1937*[60]

Most Americans paid little attention to the gloomy weather that came with the first day of 1937. After seven years of economic depression, they had more immediate worries about jobs, homes and the welfare of their families as well as events around the country and the world. They followed stories in the press about striking autoworkers, the president's battle with the Supreme Court and the Spanish civil war. They kept up with the events of the day but few realized the extraordinary events in motion far above the Ohio Valley in the gray and cloudy skies.

A cold front hung over the Pacific states, the plateau and Rocky Mountain regions, the plains states and the upper Mississippi Valley. Normally, areas of high pressure such as this rotate toward the east but this one remained stationary. At the same time, another stationary cold front hovered over an area from the south Atlantic states, the eastern part of the Gulf of Mexico and over the Bahamas and Bermuda. Its pressure distribution resulted in a continuous northward and northeastward movement of tropical air masses over Louisiana and Tennessee eastward toward New England. As it moved north, this warm moist air collided with the cold front over the Ohio and Mississippi Valleys, resulting in a colossal rainstorm. A *Time* magazine reporter stated: "Instead of remaining on the ground as snow and draining gradually, the winter precipitation had fallen as cold rain, millions of tons of it; to make a wet and gloomy hell of high water as the swollen torrent swept nine-hundred miles south-west through ten sodden states."[61]

The U.S. Weather Service estimated that over 165 billion tons of water fell in these areas in January alone. During the night of January 1, rainfall amounts exceeded four inches at some points, causing already swollen rivers in the Cumberland and Tennessee River basins to quickly flood. As early as January 8, portions of the lower reaches of the Ohio River rose above flood stage from the mouth at Cairo, Illinois, back to Paducah, Kentucky. Rivers nearly reached flood stages from Paducah to Louisville, and the Ohio was one-half to two-thirds full all the way to Pittsburgh. Brown, frothy water from the long, wide rivers of the Ohio and central Mississippi systems crept up the banks, reaching the sides of the levees, spilling over the top and then surging into the river towns. The floodwater killed 58 people, forced over 500,000 people from their homes and destroyed millions of dollars of property in an area of twenty thousand square miles.[62]

The rain increased in intensity as the month wore on with the worst on January 13, 14 and 17. The storms hit the lower Ohio Valley hardest with four times its normal precipitation. The ground lacked absorbency because of deforestation, excess water and seasonal cold temperatures, causing rapid runoff into streams and rivers already overburdened due to the previous heavy December rains. To make matters worse, the heaviest rains fell on or near the Ohio River and the mouths of its tributaries. This caused the river to fill to capacity quickly and reach flood stage from Cairo, Illinois, to Cincinnati, Ohio, by January 18.[63]

West Virginia took the flood's brunt in the upper Ohio Valley. The Red Cross ordered Wheeling Island's ten thousand residents to evacuate as the Ohio River submerged the island under a forty-seven-foot crest. Flooded roads left bus and trolley service virtually useless, and the Baltimore and Ohio Railroad suspended operation on its Ohio division. The high water crippled mills and flooded mines, leaving thirty thousand jobless. Flooding drove thousands from their homes in the one-hundred-mile area between Parkersburg and Huntington. Stores closed and trucks hauled everything movable back into the hills while churches and synagogues became rescue stations and refugee barracks.[64]

By the morning of January 24—Black Sunday—record-setting flooding along the Ohio River extended to Portsmouth, Ohio. The river first broke all records established during the 1913 flood and then proceeded to top the even more disastrous inundations of 1884. In 1930, engineers erected a steel and concrete sea wall as protection from the Scioto and Ohio Rivers. In 1936, they extended the flood works with a sixty-two-foot wall to bolster the existing earthen levee. Even so, no one planned for a flood like this, and the impressive works proved no match for the flood. City Manager Frank Sheehan ordered sirens and factory whistles sounded as the National Guard and other relief agencies evacuated twenty-five thousand inhabitants to Chillicothe and Columbus.[65]

Twenty feet of water covered Cincinnati's wholesale and tenement district, known as the Bottoms. City officials closed schools and used the buildings as shelter in order to bed, feed and provide typhoid inoculations for the forty thousand homeless. Not all residents of the Bottoms got away safely; a house with five screaming people in it fell into the raging Ohio as onlookers stood helplessly on the bank. The Norfolk and Western Railroad shut down when floods east of the city washed out tracks at Clear Creek near the Little Miami River. Other lines closed when backwater submerged the new Union Station tracks in old Mill Creek Valley. An even greater danger threatened the waterfront when oil tanks in Mill Creek Valley tore loose from their foundations and began floating around and leaking their contents in the rising waters. The following day a spark ignited twenty-five thousand gallons of gasoline floating in the Ohio River. A floating inferno over eight stories high swept over a three-mile front causing the evacuation of over forty homes.[66]

Radio station WHAS gave the nation front-row seats to the unfolding disaster in Louisville, Kentucky. Sitting on low ground where the Ohio drops twenty-six feet in two miles, Louisville residents watched the city's west end sink under the yellow torrent, driving 200,000 from their homes. The flood disrupted telephone service and city officials put residents on a two-hour water ration each day. Health workers set up two typhoid inoculation stations as sewage backed up in the municipal disposal system. Bus and trolley service ceased, leaving the Southern Railroad as the only means of transportation out of town. Electric generating plants by the river faltered and then quit, plunging the city's residents into darkness. All police remained on twenty-four hour duty and companies of National Guardsmen arrived to help them maintain order. Governor Albert Benjamin "Happy" Chandler declared martial law and telephoned President Franklin D. Roosevelt requesting federal troops to help out. Two-thirds of Louisville's residents had already fled when emergency workers evacuated the remaining 100,000 residents on January 25 after floodwater made its way into the central business district.[67]

Riots broke out in Kentucky at the Frankfort Reformatory when its nearly three thousand prisoners awoke to water in their cells. Governor Chandler entered the gates in an outboard motorboat. Inmates called out "Get us out of here, Happy! We're gonna drown if you don't!" Chandler replied: "It's a hell of a mess, boys, but I'm going to get you out and take care of you!" Chandler promises offered little consolation and the prisoners panicked. Twenty-five tried to escape by swimming out into the river, but all but one returned when guards fired shots over their heads. At first, everybody fought the guards but then the prisoners split along racial lines and fought each other. The chaos overwhelmed the National Guardsmen sent to quell the riot. They withdrew outside the prison walls, announcing that twelve prisoners were dead and that all had "absolutely gone mad." Chandler telephoned Washington for not only troops but also doctors from the U.S. Public Health Service to help set up a prison camp on the State Insane Asylum Grounds. As many as one hundred either died in the melee or drowned before National Guardsmen eventually put down the uprising.[68]

The Cumberland River and its tributaries overflowed and flooded much of Middle Tennessee. On January 17, police issued flood warnings to residents in low-lying areas of Nashville, Tennessee. The Cumberland River reached an all-time high of sixty-two feet, twenty-four feet above flood stage at Clarkesville. The sudden and overwhelming flooding caused the drowning of numerous people, including Clyde Davis who fell out of an ambulance and drowned in the Obion River near Huntingdon while taking his father to a hospital and Earl Kilgore who drowned when his car was caught in a swollen creek.[69]

Flooding continued as the Ohio River's flood stage broke all previous records. The crest reached 19.6 feet above flood stage at Cairo, 3.2 feet above the previous high. The river at Louisville, Kentucky, swelled from 51.5 feet to 54.8 feet. It climbed to 30 feet above flood stage by January 26, breaking the previous record by 11 feet. The stage at Cincinnati rose from 73.4 to 78.7 feet and eventually reached 80 feet by January 26, breaking the existing record by 28 feet. The Red Cross ordered residents out of Paducah on January 24 after floodwater reached the depth of 8 feet downtown. Over a thousand families abandoned their flooded homes in low-lying areas of Pittsburgh, and residents in Cairo nervously waited for the U.S Army Corps of Engineers to activate the Bird's Point–New Madrid Floodway as the flood stage reached a record 58.6 feet.[70]

The destruction spread as the floodwater moved toward the Gulf of Mexico. Even before the floodwater arrived, the same weather system that soaked the Ohio Valley also inundated eastern Arkansas, the Missouri boot heel, north Mississippi, western Kentucky and western Tennessee, raising the waters of many Mississippi River tributaries. Just as the Ohio Valley, conditions in the mid-South appeared ripe for disaster. On January 8, conditions took a turn for the worse as the rain that pummeled the region turned to sleet and snow after a sudden thirty-degree drop in temperature. Precipitation continued and by January 11 the White and Black Rivers in Arkansas rose above flood marks in several places. Residents living near the St. Francis River near Paragould, Arkansas, began to evacuate as water reached their homes. Continued rains in Arkansas caused the waters of the St. Francis, Ouachita, White, Black and Little Rivers to go as high as seven feet over flood stage in places. Floodwater washed out twelve state highways and Greene County's Big Slough levee ruptured, flooding thousands of acres of rich farmland.[71]

Southeast Missouri residents faced worsening conditions as well. By January 11, the St. Francis River climbed to 23.7 feet at Fisk, Missouri. Governor Lloyd C. Stark ordered a refugee camp set up for fifty families fleeing the threatened area; two hundred more were expected by morning. The next day, weather bureaus in St. Louis and Memphis warned that rainfall and melting sleet would cause the Black and St. Francis Rivers in southeast Missouri to "go on flood rampages" within thirty-six hours. Army engineers tried to save the St. Francis River levees in Missouri but, in the face of rising water, ordered their fifteen hundred workers and their families to flee for their lives.[72]

The weakening levees fueled suspicion and fears of sabotage. On January 13, Governor Stark ordered Missouri National Guardsmen to patrol the

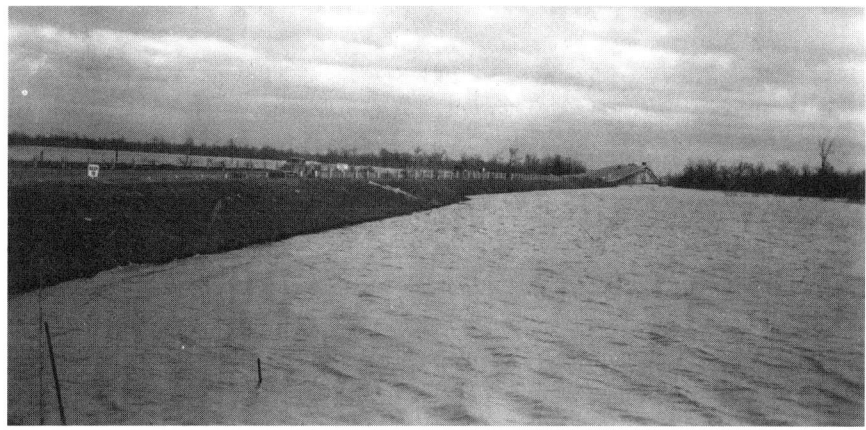

Highway 70 near West Memphis. *Courtesy of the Memphis and Shelby County Room, Memphis Public Library and Information Center.*

straining levees along the Black River south of Poplar Bluff in search of leaks and saboteurs. By January 16, armed patrols monitoring the levees around Big Lake and the Little River in Arkansas had orders to shoot anyone caught tampering with their levees. At Blytheville, guards posted on the Mississippi levees received orders to shoot to kill any Tennessean who crossed the river to dynamite the levee to save his land.[73]

The Tennessee militia had the same orders to keep Arkansans and Missourians from sabotaging Tennessee levees. Acting secretary and brother of the governor, F.L. Browning asked Governor Gordon Browning, who was still in Washington, for permission to mobilize the state militia. On January 22, a unit of the Tennessee National Guard arrived to patrol the levees near Tiptonville because of rumors of Missouri residents planning to dynamite the levee. Lieutenant Ray C. Reeves broadcast a call to Shelby County guardsmen to assemble at the fairgrounds armory in Memphis. Once assembled, Colonel W.L. Terry ordered the 180 men of the 115th Field Artillery to proceed to Dyersburg. They joined 50 National Guardsmen of the 117th Infantry from Jackson under the command of Colonel R.H. Bond to guard the levee in Dyersburg between Tiptonville and Hickman, Kentucky.[74]

The troops from Memphis kept the levee secure and maintained order throughout the flood. The situation became especially difficult after two tremors struck the area that "adding to the terrors of residents." Some feared more might follow and cause the levees to fail or create another lake like Reelfoot, which formed as a result of a series of earthquakes that shook the Mississippi Valley between mid-December 1811 and mid-March 1812. The levees stood up to the quakes but not the river. By February 3, water from the Mississippi River had made its way through numerous breaks in the levees near Bessie, Tennessee, and surrounded Tiptonville.[75]

Tributaries in northern Mississippi and west Tennessee flooded as well. Water from the overflowing Tallahatchie and Coldwater Rivers spilled into homes and plantations in low-lying areas. By January 17, those rising rivers began to threaten Tate, Quitman and Panola Counties. West Tennessee residents watched as nearby tributaries backed up and overflowed. The Wolf River, North Fork River and streams in Fayette County flooded hundreds of acres of farmlands. Dyer County residents evacuated when the Forked Deer River flooded, and floodwater caused fifteen freight cars to derail on the L&N railroad tracks between Paris and Clarksville.[76]

During the first week of January, rising waters did not cause a great deal of concern in Memphis because, as a *Time* magazine reporter wrote that

High Water Blues

"in the past eight years the Army's brains and Congressional generosity have provided the Mississippi with a flood control system whose limits will supposedly never be approached." U.S. Army Corps of Engineers made significant improvements following the Mississippi Valley Flood of 1927 and they had great confidence in the new flood-control measures. District engineer lieutenant colonel Eugene Reybold stated that the levees of the Memphis district, which extended from Cairo to Helena, could easily withstand the predicted thirty-four-foot flood stage. In fact, recently inaugurated Governor Gordon Browning left his office in the care of aides, as did the most important political leaders in Memphis. Ed Crump, still at the Sugar Bowl game in New Orleans, sent his most trusted lieutenant, Frank Rice, to the Tennessee General Assembly. On January 18, the recently divorced Mayor Watkins Overton married his longtime secretary, Bessie Ganong. After the ten-minute ceremony at the Second Presbyterian Church, the two went on a northern honeymoon, leaving Commissioner Clifford Davis in charge until his return.[77]

The situation changed in a matter of days as news spread of the overflowing tributaries in eastern Arkansas. Radio reports from the Ohio Valley gave ominous warnings of what lay ahead for the Mississippi Valley as the flood crest headed toward Cairo. Officials worried that they faced a repeat of the flood of 1927 and began to prepare for the worst by using the same basic organizational scheme used ten years earlier. Mayor Overton put his honeymoon on hold and hurried back to Memphis to relieve Davis. On January 20, Overton and Shelby County chairman E.W. Hale received extraordinary powers by their respective governments to deal with the crisis. They created the Mayor's Disaster Committee, consisting of Red Cross, city officials, representatives from the county government and the local American Legion to create a comprehensive plan to handle relief efforts and immediate flood control.[78]

Federal, state and local officials wasted little time in coordinating efforts by using the 1927 relief operations and a model. National Red Cross disaster director George Myer arrived in Memphis on January 20 to establish a regional headquarters in order to supervise relief efforts for Tennessee, Mississippi, Louisiana and Alabama. Local Red Cross chairman Clinton Schley, who initially sent Arkansans seeking aid back to their community Red Cross chapters, now took charge of general preparations for large-scale refugee relief and handled the shortage of supplies in anticipation of large numbers of refugees. Chairman John Ross and Director Sam Jackson offered the services of the Memphis Welfare Committee (MWC) and its remaining money and food supplies intended for those on relief rolls.[79]

Memphis and the Superflood of 1937

On January 23, the *Commercial Appeal* stated:

> *Heightened by twenty-four-hour rains over a watershed of a dozen states, the greatest flood in the history of the Ohio Valley is roaring southward today aiming its full force against the levees on the lower Mississippi which U.S. Engineers declare with confidence will be able to withstand the terrific pounding.*

Even so, they knew they would face a disaster like the 1927 flood if the untested flood-control measures failed. Meteorologists predicted a forty-four-foot flood stage as water rushed toward the St. Francis levee three miles away from the banks of the Mississippi. Local officials knew that they might face battles on several fronts: caring for the refugees arriving by the hundreds by the hour, organizing efforts to rescue those stranded in flooded areas and protecting the city from the floodwater.[80]

The flood not only threatened Memphis physically but it also endangered the credibility of Ed Crump and the local political machine. Politicians not only prided themselves on their secure positions and influence throughout the state and over the White House, but they also understood the precarious nature of power. Flood damage to new industry would mean the loss of revenue and jobs as well as discouraging other much-needed businesses from locating in Memphis. Failing to provide for the local population and large numbers refugees could have forced the machine to relinquish control of relief efforts and reconstruction to federal authorities. Direct aid that bypassed local governmental agencies would have meant the loss of control of federal money and the ability to award jobs based on loyalty to the machine. The machine at least had to appear to remain viable or risk losing the public confidence needed to maintain its ironclad rule of the city.

HIGH WATER BLUES

*Down at the Fairgrounds on my knees
Prayin' to the Lord to give me ease
Lord, Lord, I got them high water blues.
—Unknown artist, 1937*[81]

The new mainline levees held back the overflow from the Mississippi River, but many smaller levees along the tributaries could not contain backwater from the main channel. Once these levees broke, people in the low-lying areas had very little time to react. The water rose so rapidly that many escaped with little more than the clothes on their backs. Others managed to bring what possessions and livestock they could carry in trucks, cars or wagons. Adding to the misery, refugees often became sick from outbreaks of influenza and pneumonia brought by the sudden drops in temperature. Many sought refuge in nearby Red Cross camps but many more, remembering the hardships of the 1927 flood, headed directly to Memphis.

W.C. Cornelius and his family narrowly escaped from their home near Steele, Missouri. He told a newspaper reporter at Ellis Auditorium on January 24 that "from Friday afternoon [January 22] until we left our home Saturday morning I would have rather been dead than alive." In the days prior to their escape, Cornelius, his wife and fourteen-year-old son anxiously listened to WMC radio broadcasts hoping that a rescue boat would save them from the flood. When the freezing water pushed through their floor they realized they could no longer wait for help and tried to leave. They rushed from the house but the rising water quickly overwhelmed them. Cornelius called out to a neighbor across the flooded field struggling to save his mules from the neck-deep frozen water. He spotted the stricken and used his boat to carry them to a nearby levee. From there, Cornelius and his family walked to Steele and eventually made it to Memphis, arriving cold, sick and with feet cut from walking across miles of broken ice.[82]

Floodwater quickly engulfed a hollow in east Arkansas near the Tyronza River where Ed Brooks, his wife and seven children worked a farm. They waded through the icy overflowing river until they reached high ground. At times, the father had to carry three of his children while the mother had to carry their six-month-old child over her head through waist-deep water. After they finally reached safety, they rode in a freezing boxcar to Memphis. After arriving at the train station, Red Cross workers took them to Ellis Auditorium where they received blankets and slept on the concrete floor.[83]

Thousands of others with similar stories soon arrived in need of help. The Mayor's Disaster Committee met on January 22 and selected the fairgrounds park once again as the site for the refugee camp and charged the American Legion, under the direction of Commander Frank Gailor, with feeding, housing and setting up the proper facilities for five thousand people.

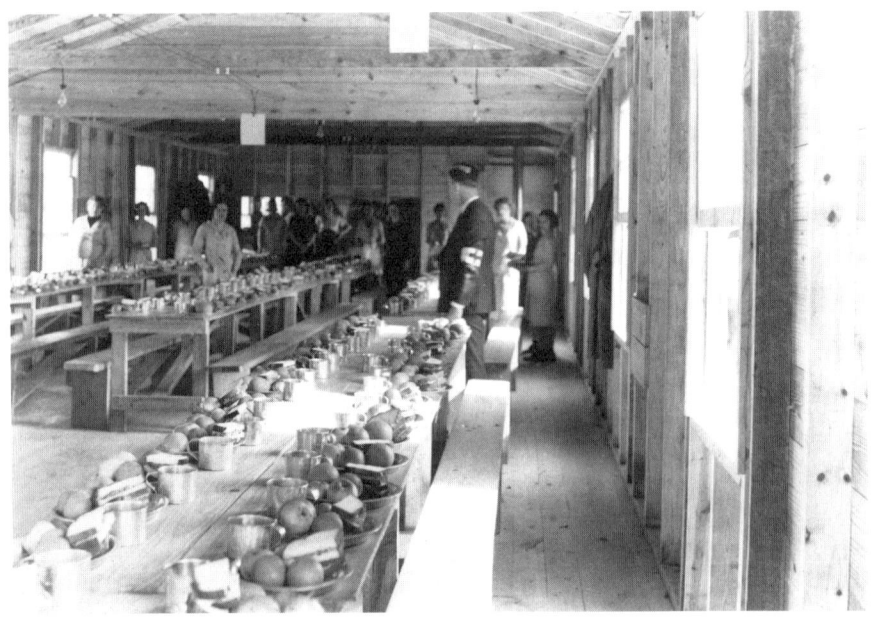

Food prepared by WPA for refugees at the fairgrounds. *Courtesy of the Memphis and Shelby County Room, Memphis Public Library and Information Center.*

High Water Blues

D. Eugene "Gene" Wagner, local Red Cross president, and Frank Grout, head of Colonial Baking Company and chairman of roll call, organized eight hundred workers to provide food for refugees. Workers connected light circuits to allow crews to continue their work through the night as they quickly equipped the existing buildings with mobile kitchens and cots with blankets. Twenty union volunteers constructed thirty-by-four-foot tables for the mess halls in the rooms behind the Women's Building. Electricians and gas crews installed fixtures for lighting and cooking under the supervision of park commission superintendent Dave Renfrow and Ike Friedman, vice chairman of the American Legion Disaster and Relief Committee.[84]

The local Works Progress Administration (WPA) under S. Tate Pease provided crucial workers for all aspects of relief and flood control. They built up levees, maintained the fairgrounds camp, cared for refugees and even manufactured goods to replace those lost in the flood. In addition, WPA workers interacted with refugees as maids, orderlies, cooks and daycare workers.

The fairgrounds transformed nearly overnight to accommodate the expected five thousand flood victims. The American Legion segregated the

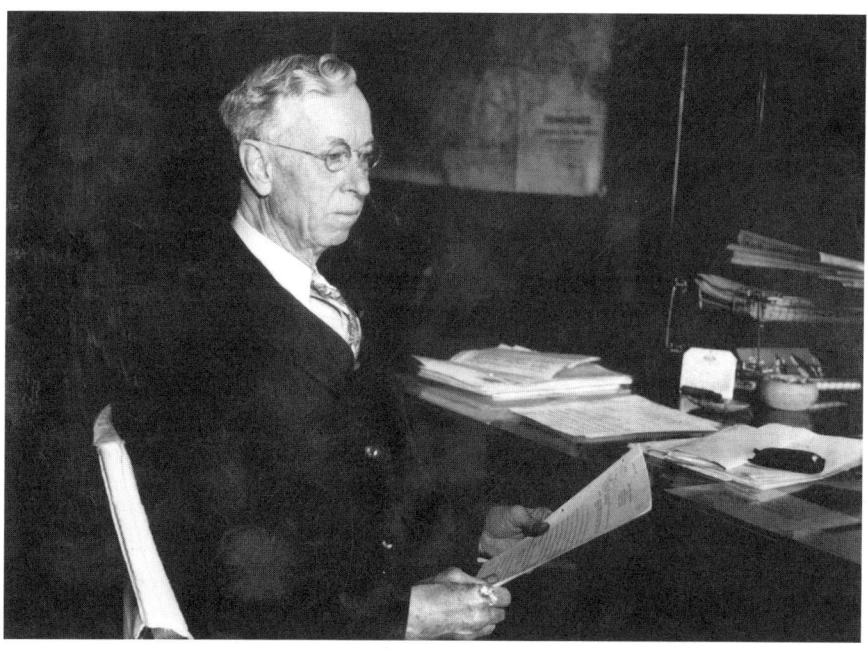

Memphis WPA director S. Tate Pease. *Courtesy of the Memphis and Shelby County Room, Memphis Public Library and Information Center.*

Memphis and the Superflood of 1937

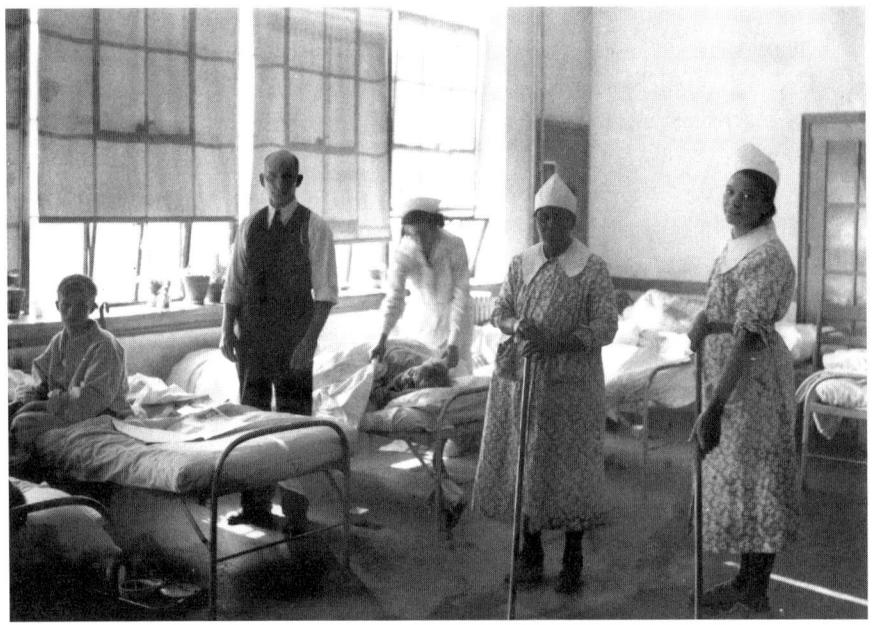

WPA maids and orderlies care for sick refugees. *Courtesy of the Memphis and Shelby County Room, Memphis Public Library and Information Center.*

refugees by gender and race: they housed white women in the Merchant's Building, white men in the Automobile Building, African American women in the Educational Building and African American men in the Cattle Building. The first-aid building became the medical center; church booths became mess halls; officials took registrations at the cattle barn; and the Lee Lumber Company building became the headquarters. W.O. "Barney" Butler, chairman of the Red Cross lifesaving unit, remembered that husbands and wives complained about the separate housing but, for the most part, people made the best of the situation. "The kids thought it was a picnic," Butler remembered. "Some of the people brought banjos and guitars out with them and there was music." WPA recreation directors and Junior Red Cross workers arranged entertainment for the refugees under the supervision of the Memphis Park Commission while local church congregations helped provide supplies. They had children's outdoor games, kite making, movies, vaudeville shows, quilting for women, checkers for men, daily concerts and even the Municipal Circus helped out. Workers at the emergency quarters at Third and Jefferson Avenue made clothing, rugs and toys under the supervision of WPA administrator Ethel Dick. The WPA also made up

High Water Blues

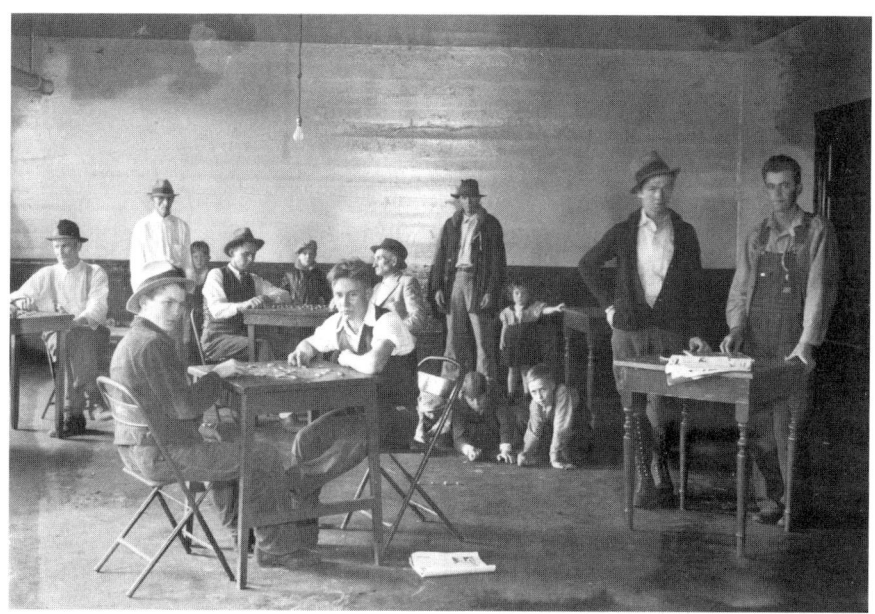

Refugee men playing checkers while some boys play marbles. *Courtesy of the Memphis and Shelby County Room, Memphis Public Library and Information Center.*

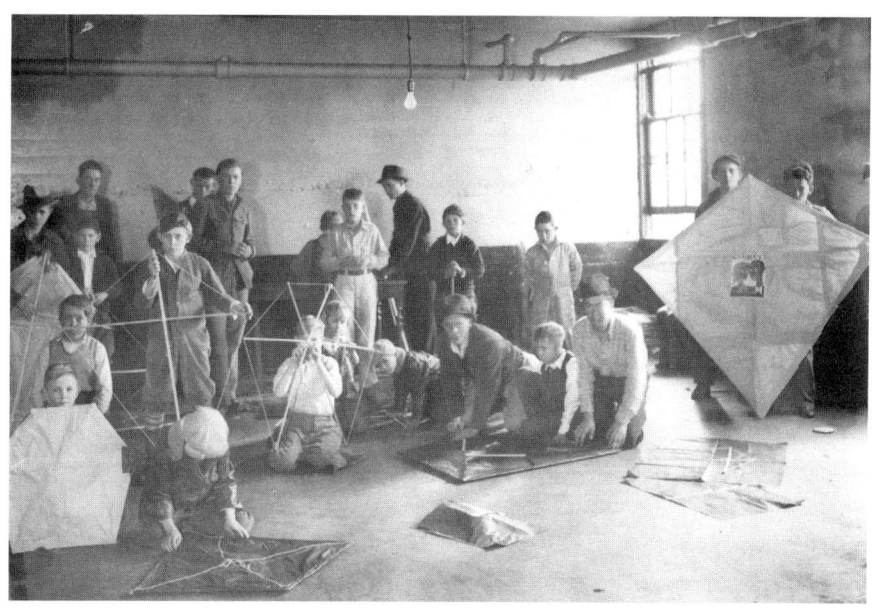

The WPA included kite making as a recreational activity for the refugees. *Courtesy of the Memphis and Shelby County Room, Memphis Public Library and Information Center.*

Memphis and the Superflood of 1937

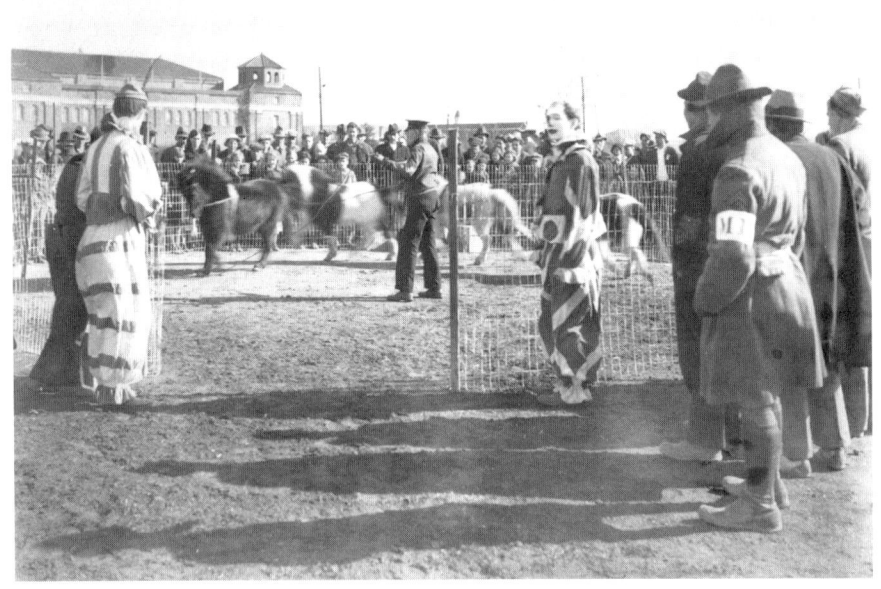

The Memphis Municipal Circus performs for the refugees at the fairgrounds. *Courtesy of the Memphis and Shelby County Room, Memphis Public Library and Information Center.*

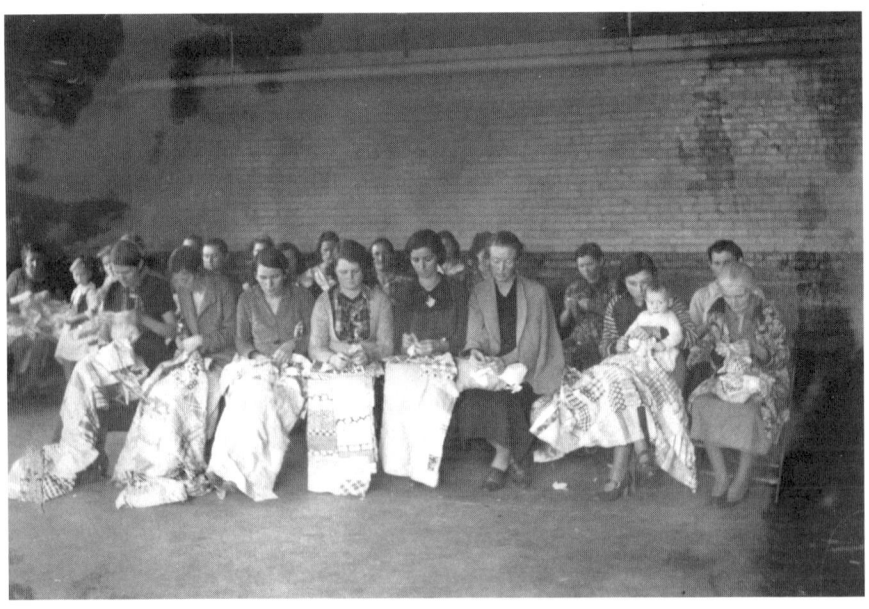

Refugee women spent free time making quilts from materials donated by churches and other organizations. *Courtesy of the Memphis and Shelby County Room, Memphis Public Library and Information Center.*

High Water Blues

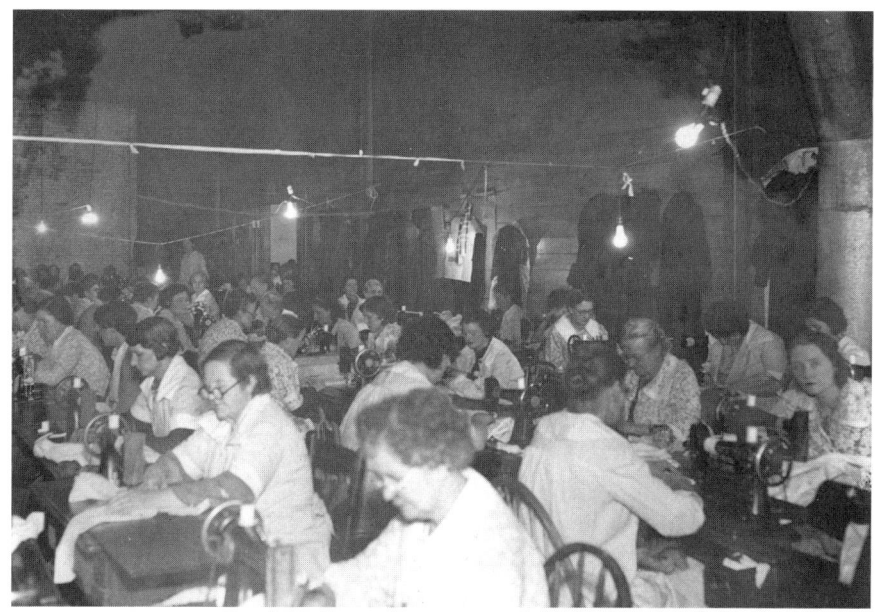

WPA garment workers prepare clothing for refugees. *Courtesy of the Memphis and Shelby County Room, Memphis Public Library and Information Center.*

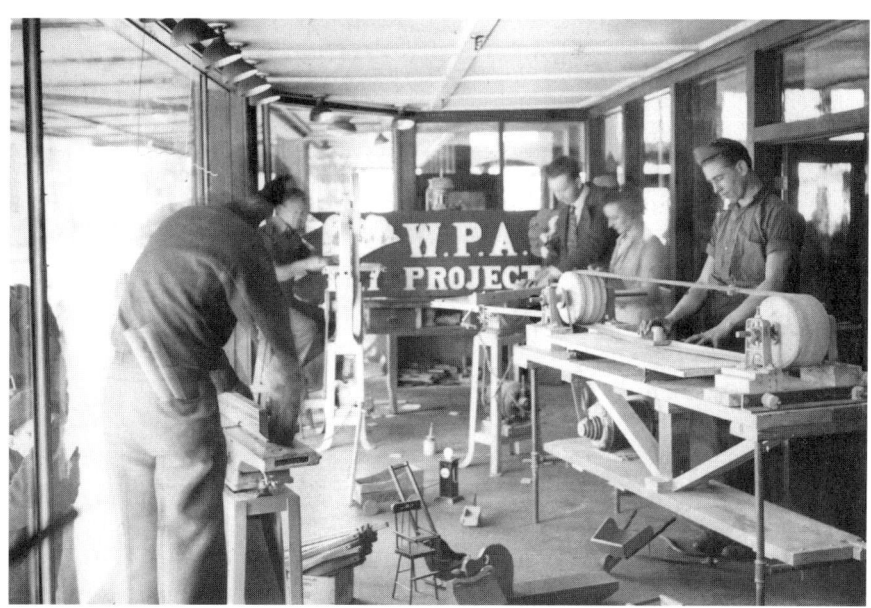

WPA workers make toys for refugee children to replace those lost in the flood. *Courtesy of the Memphis and Shelby County Room, Memphis Public Library and Information Center.*

sunshine packages containing donated toys, magazines and books for the children in the refugee centers.[85]

The disaster committee faced an unexpected shortage of cots because the local Red Cross sent the ones normally kept at the Ellis Auditorium to tornado-ravaged Tupelo, Mississippi, the previous spring. City Attorney Will Gerber telephoned Congressman Walter Chandler in Washington asking him to contact the Army and request that the local National Guard give their five hundred cots and blankets stored at the Fairgrounds to the refugees. On January 23, Governor Browning returned to Nashville from Washington and also requested additional cots and tents from the War Department for the refugees in west Tennessee. Bedding for five thousand soon arrived at the Memphis fairgrounds, included cots, sleeping bags and empty mattresses that refugees could stuff with straw or hay.[86]

Memphis clothier Julius Lewis found out about the shortage and stepped in to help out. The Red Cross needed single blankets for emergency shelters in the schools and the fairgrounds as local supplies had run out. Meanwhile cold and wet refugees continued to stream into Memphis. While relief workers waited for the delivery from the War Department, Lewis bought the more expensive doubles, carefully cut them in half and gave them to the Red Cross.[87]

Meanwhile, the flooding worsened beyond all expectations in eastern Arkansas, and it soon became apparent that Memphians would have to care for far more refugees than anticipated. The large numbers of refugees soon overwhelmed the processing center. On January 26, as the flood crest moved south from the Ohio Valley, officials in Washington told the Red Cross at Memphis to prepare the city for fifty thousand refugees, ten times the number city officials originally expected. Mayor Overton met the next day with the disaster committee to come up with a strategy to handle the increase of refugees, though he doubted the city could care for that many people. Relief officials immediately ordered more barracks and mess halls built at the fairgrounds, and the Legionnaires made an appeal to Memphians for additional stoves for cooking and heat. Even so, camp officials could barely keep pace with the new arrivals and soon faced numerous sanitation and safety issues.[88]

Health workers made every effort to inoculate the healthy and quarantine the sick but the hundreds of refugees arriving in Memphis by the hour strained the fairgrounds' facilities. According to city and county health authorities, the congestion of flood refugees, sick with "almost every type of communicable disease," presented the greatest health hazard since the influenza epidemic of 1918. Typical refugees arriving at the fairgrounds went to the cattle barns for registration where they received paper identification tags on strings to hang around their necks and a series of inoculations, many personally given by Dr. L.M. Graves. National Youth Administration (NYA) workers handed out new blankets and quilts to replace the bedding confiscated at registration, gave new clothes and assigned cots.[89]

The fairgrounds camp held over eighty-five hundred by January 28, making even basic registration difficult. In response, the disaster committee changed the processing procedures so that new arrivals went to Ellis Auditorium for registrations and medical examinations before transportation to the proper facility. The refugees received their first of three vaccinations for smallpox and typhoid fever when they arrived at Ellis. Medical personnel gave the remaining shots once the refugees arrived at the fairgrounds or other relief centers. In addition, they immunized children against diphtheria and set up sanitary patrols and isolation wards for anyone with a communicable disease.[90]

On January 27, Red Cross director George Myer assigned Dr. Marion S. Lombard of the Marine Hospital in Memphis to supervise all health activities

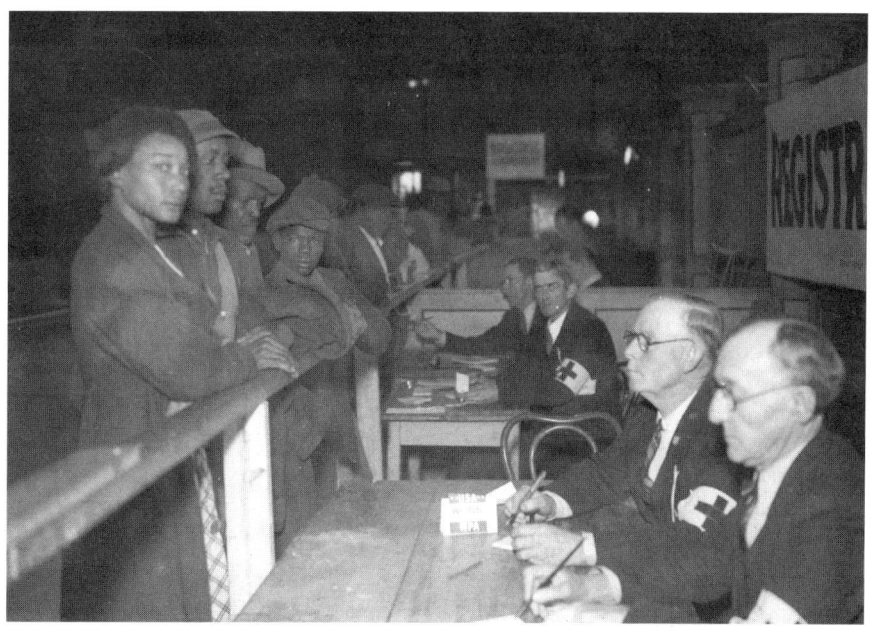

Refugee registration at Ellis Auditorium. *Courtesy of the Memphis and Shelby County Room, Memphis Public Library and Information Center.*

in the city. Lombard's recent experience overseeing the refugee camp at Mayfield, Kentucky, for the twenty thousand Paducah refugees helped prepare him for the unfolding crisis in Memphis. He cleared the fairgrounds first-aid clinic of the more than five hundred cases of severe colds and about fifty cases of pneumonia. Once local hospitals filled to capacity, Lombard directed Red Cross, city officials, health authorities and the Memphis and Shelby County Medical Society to set up hospital equipment in every available school and church. They moved patients to Memphis Eye, Ear, Nose and Throat Hospital, the Juvenile Court Building, the Orange Mound School and the old Shelby County Hospital on Raleigh Road. Crews set up six hundred beds at Fairview Junior High over two days while the regular cafeteria staff stayed to feed patients. Lawler School in Binghamton and Tech High School hospitalized whites, and Carnes School on Lane Street and Booker T. Washington High School took African American patients. By January 28, the maternity ward at the Ella Oliver Home had ten patients and Juvenile Court held thirty-nine babies and five mothers.[91]

The WPA Women's Professional Projects, under west Tennessee director Virginia Robinson, provided additional personnel to receive,

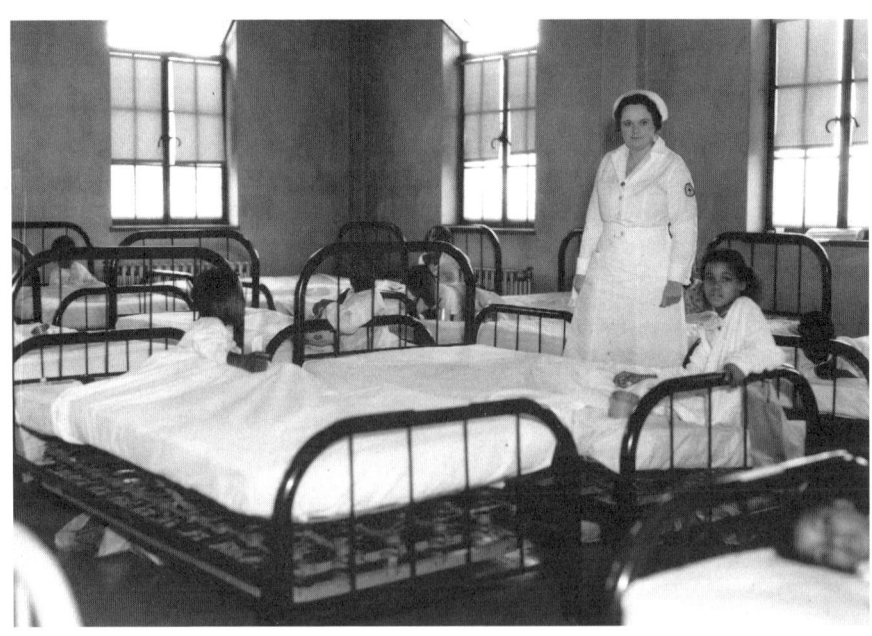

Sick children in the Red Cross hospital set up in the Juvenile Court Building. *Courtesy of the Memphis and Shelby County Room, Memphis Public Library and Information Center.*

High Water Blues

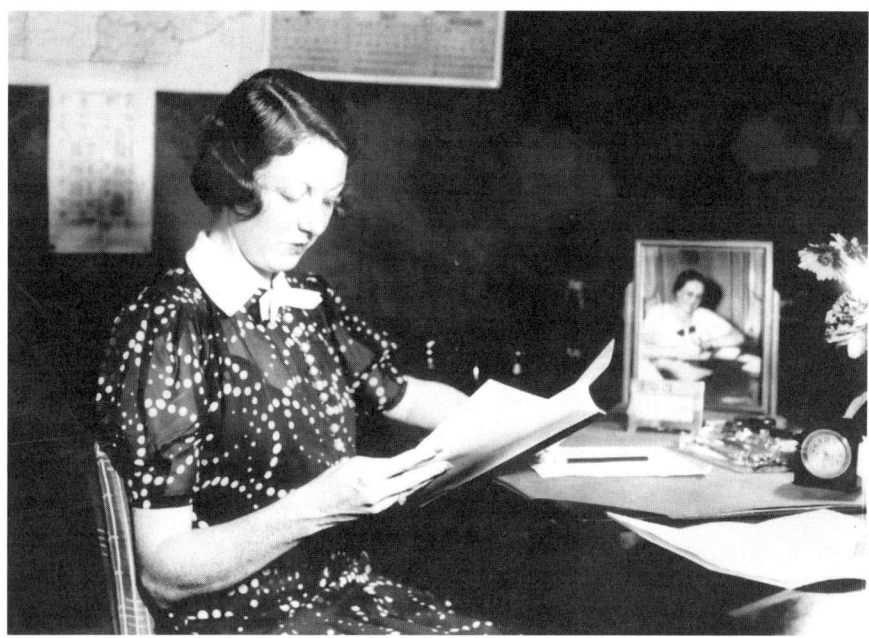

Virginia Robinson of the WPA. *Courtesy of the Memphis and Shelby County Room, Memphis Public Library and Information Center.*

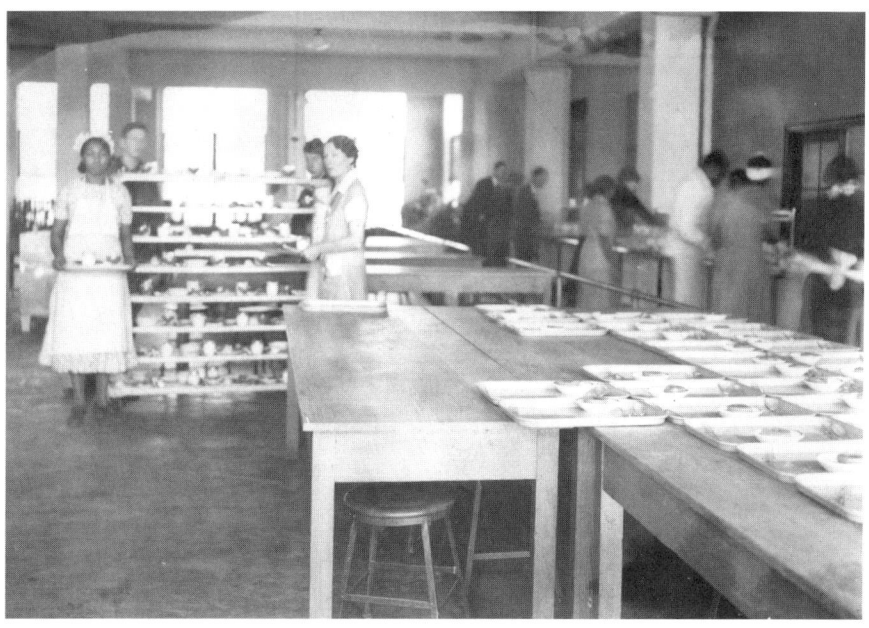

WPA workers prepare food trays for patients at Fairview School. *Courtesy of the Memphis and Shelby County Room, Memphis Public Library and Information Center.*

care for and distribute refugees. WPA workers served as registers and transported refugees to local hospitals, private homes and camps. They also provided kitchen maids, orderlies, nursing assistants, waitresses, linen room attendants and general help while National Youth Administration (NYA) workers and Boy Scouts became runners, doormen, postmen and aides at hospitals.[92]

The disaster committee made every effort to accommodate the refugees but, at the same time, the growing concern over a possible epidemic led city officials to keep arriving refugees virtual prisoners in the refugee centers. Mayor Overton ordered flood-relief organizations to supervise all flood victims coming to Memphis to make sure they stayed off the streets. The National Guard "threw a tight military cordon" around the twelve thousand refugees already in Memphis and enforced strict rules regarding access to the fairgrounds and other recently opened relief centers. Only people with pass cards issued by the American Legion or Red Cross could enter the fairgrounds, and guards prohibited automobiles from entering the camps unless used by staff. Luggage remained in a separate building that the owners could only access with a special emergency permit in order to prevent the spread of disease. Men could not enter in the women's quarters after 4:00

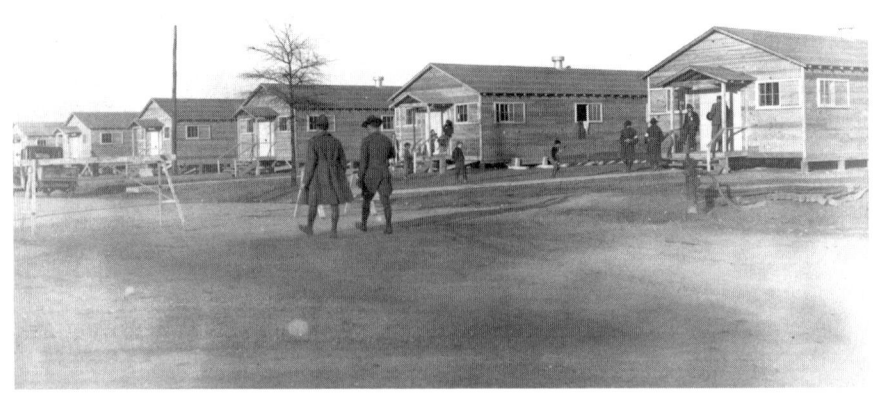

State militia patrols barracks at the fairgrounds. *Courtesy of the Memphis and Shelby County Room, Memphis Public Library and Information Center.*

p.m., and refugees could not leave the camp unless to transfer to the homes of friends or relatives in Memphis or to other facilities.[93]

Camp officials narrowly avoided tragedy when a fire broke out in the early morning on January 28. The Automobile Building did not have a chimney, so refugees knocked out windowpanes to vent the stoves used to provide heat. The heaters soon overwhelmed the makeshift ventilation system and caused a fire along the overheated wall. Nearly two thousand men housed in the building woke to smoke and flames at about 5:00 a.m. Fortunately, Commissioner Davis had ordered a detachment of one hundred firemen to remain on twenty-four-hour duty at the camp only hours earlier. Fire captain Joe Schaefer and his men quickly put out the fire and saved the refugees in the building.[94]

Most refugees crossing the Harahan Bridge gladly followed the line of arrows tacked up by ROTC students leading them to Ellis Auditorium but others refused to cooperate. Many hoped to avoid confinement in the camps and possible relocation. Truckloads of people arrived in Memphis and scattered into surrounding buildings and alleyways, causing concern about the spread of contagious diseases. At the time, officials believed as many as twenty thousand unvaccinated refugees roamed the streets. The police rounded up those found without verification of inoculation and took them to Ellis Auditorium where Shelby County Red Cross director W.I. Jones had set up a new registration center. Once they arrived at the fairgrounds, some hid in bushes or in corners of buildings to avoid transportation out of town. At one point, workers found a mother and her two children in a pile of Cotton Carnival decorations. To their relief, they only had to relocate to Central High School rather than out of the city.[95]

The problems did not end there; petty criminals either took advantage of relief services or tried to swindle refugees. A city court judge fined four Memphians caught working the "rackets" at the Red Cross relief station in Ellis Auditorium on February 5 on charges of vagrancy and disorderly conduct. C.A. Webb, who police referred to as a "professional hobo," received a sixty-dollar fine after he forged a pass for admittance to the Ellis Auditorium for meals and lodging reserved for refugees. Arthur Grover drew a thirty-five-dollar fine when he admitted he obtained free lodging and meals as a relief worker without doing any work. Rex Brown received a sixty-dollar fine after he offered free lodging to fellow African Americans fleeing floodwater but then demanding the victims' Red Cross food orders as rent. While cooking at Ellis Auditorium, Walter J. Lucas also prepared steaks for employees in the refugee clothing department, who then showed their appreciation by giving Lucas several suits of clothes and six pairs of shoes.

Judge Carter gave six more chiselers one hour to leave town after police arrested them for posing as flood victims.[96]

Congressman Walter Chandler wrote:

> *The lame, the sick, and the weary faltered on the roadside, over-laden vehicles failed under the loads and jammed the highways for hours, while shrewd traders, taking advantage of misery and distress, bought livestock and household effects from refugees at grossly inadequate prices.*

Some posed as relief workers and charged refugees to move livestock across the river, while others simply stole from them or looted their abandoned homes. Others would tell those traveling to Memphis that the city had no facilities for housing livestock in order to buy the refugees' cattle for a dollar each and chickens for a nickel. Only after the refugees made it to Ellis Auditorium did they realize the buyers swindled them. "Beale Street conmen" sold refugees arriving by train at Union Station phony relief tickets to receive Red Cross aid.[97]

Once word of these activities spread, Professor Walter W. Gibson organized some of his students, with the consent of police and relief officials, to help the refugees. Gibson, a biology instructor at the African American LeMoyne College, directed his students to meet arriving refugees to give them proper information about the housing of livestock, forcing the charlatans operating at the Harahan Bridge to give up their ruse. LeMoyne football players physically intimidated and frightened away the con men at the train station and helped direct refugees to Ellis Auditorium.[98]

Red Cross officials tried to get word out that Memphis actually had livestock holding areas available for the refugees. In fact, some landowners including L.D. Collins, L.J. Kerr, H.E. Quenichet, Frank Donelson, C.H. Schwam, Frank Podesta, F.M. Duke, J.D. Appling, Dover Barrett, Vance Norfleet, Oren Owen and Lake Hays formed a committee to see to the care of refugees' animals. They provided feed, trucks for transportation and pasture space in Shelby County and Mississippi. They even used the Desoto Fish Dock at the foot of Beale Street—the last of the old Memphis fish docks—to house a barge of one hundred cows that arrived on the morning of January 29. More help came from the Resettlement Administration under T. Roy Reid who gave farmers grants to feed their livestock, while law enforcement and concerned citizens began targeting profiteers.[99]

Refugees arrived with an assortment of strange possessions. Among the items left behind at the fairgrounds included a suitcase of century-old

High Water Blues

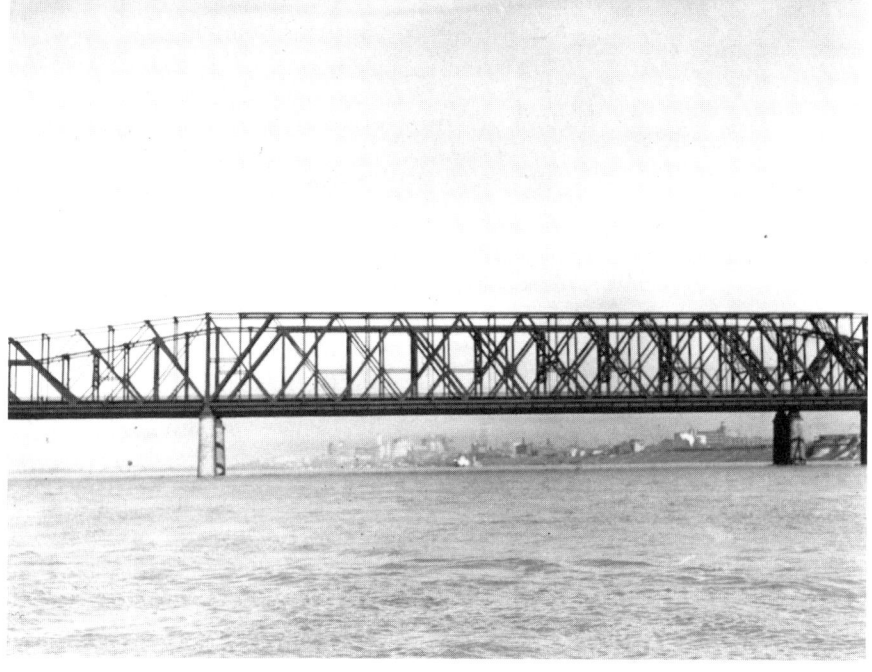

Harahan and Frisco Bridges connected Memphis to flood-ravaged eastern Arkansas. *Courtesy of the Memphis and Shelby County Room, Memphis Public Library and Information Center.*

silverware and a Confederate flag, chickens, homemade medicine and salted pork. One enterprising Arkansas refugee named S.A. Denison arrived in Memphis with the most unusual possession of all: he had what he claimed to be the corpse of Spanish explorer Hernando De Soto. The previous summer his dog unearthed a steel casket with a glass window in the lid near Denison's juke joint in the swamp near West Memphis. One of his patrons surmised it contained the body of De Soto since the Spaniard's party supposedly buried his remains in the Mississippi River. Denison erected a canvas tent over the coffin and charged a dime admission to see the famous conquistador. People sometimes asked how the explorers managed to bury De Soto in a steel coffin. Denison assured the questioning customers the conquistadors always made it a point to carry a couple of steel coffins with them during their explorations.[100]

When the area began to flood, Denison abandoned the juke joint but loaded the coffin in the back of his pickup truck and headed for Memphis. He had entertained the idea of taking the area's most famous visitor on a countrywide tour and, with his beer stand and dance floor currently underwater, it seemed like a good time to start. He rented a vacant warehouse on South Main Street and advertised his exhibit: "See the discovery of the century! See Hernando De Soto himself-in person!" To his surprise, Memphians showed little interest in his exhibit. It seems that his exhibit lacked the appeal it once had in its previous rural setting. Consequently, Denison made very little return off his investment. His situation worsened over the next several years as unpaid rent accumulated and a legal battle with a business partner dragged on. In the end, a northern investor bought the coffin and its contents and no one saw it again.[101]

The situation at the fairgrounds began to deteriorate by the end of January, leaving camp officials with no other choice but to move the refugees out. The shortage of toilets and bathing facilities for the nine thousand people interned at the camp brought about a serious breakdown in sanitation. The disaster committee could do little to remedy the situation because the overcrowding made it nearly impossible to set up new barracks, restrooms or dig drainage ditches. They searched for any available buildings to temporarily house the refugees while workers cleaned the camp. The committee closed the remaining public schools and converted them into hospitals, which quickly filled to capacity, and the Memphis Ministerial Association offered space in local churches. Officials moved about a thousand African American men to an old hospital on Raines Road and a barracks at the American Car and Foundry in Binghamton. Realtors led by Bethel T. Hunt, president of the Real Estate Board of Memphis, obtained the Ellis-Jones Building on North Court, a four-story warehouse at 61 West Georgia, and a number of other buildings and furnished houses. Despite these efforts, they could not find enough housing.[102]

Red Cross officials and the disaster committee decided the city would better serve as a receiving and distribution point for refugees rather than a long-term housing facility. Overton and Hale met at 5:00 p.m. on January 28 to make plans to get the refugees out of town, and Red Cross director Myer authorized funding for the transportation. That night, Myer and Colonel W.J. Bacon began moving healthy refugees to communities east of Memphis. The Civilian Conservation Corps (CCC) in Braden and Selmer allowed workers to return home with full pay so that their barracks could house 400 refugees. Officials moved about 450 people to Jackson, Tennessee, and Memphis Street Railway buses carried 170 more the next day. The president of the Gulf, Mobile & Northern Railroad, I.B. Tigrett offered free services to refugees going to homes of friends or relatives along the GM&N line.

High Water Blues

Officials in Tupelo, New Albany and Water Valley, Mississippi, also offered to take refugees. Officials in Birmingham, Alabama, made arrangements to take 5,000, and the Chattanooga mayor agreed to house 2,000 but they later transferred the 400 African Americans to Fort Oglethorpe, Georgia. On January 29, Bacon reported to the disaster committee that Humbolt, Counte, Shiloh, Corinth and Collierville would accept 150 refugees each; Jackson, McKenzie, Dyer, Fayetteville, Adamsville, Pickwick Dam and Lawrenceburg County would take 200 each; the town of Lawrenceburg agreed to take 400; and Tullahoma would take 2,000.[103]

Even before the meeting, Henry Baker had directed refugees back to Arkansas. Busloads of Dyess Colony refugees began arriving after Baker radioed instructions to evacuate on January 21. Musician Johnny Cash, who grew up in Dyess, recalled the Tyronza River flooding the settlement and forcing out all but a handful of residents who guarded property and tended to livestock. Volunteers transported people from their flooded homes with tractors and boats to the local community center where they boarded trucks headed for Bassett fifteen miles away. About five hundred took trains into central and western Arkansas to stay with relatives, and about a thousand others took the buses Baker arranged to carry them to Memphis. Once in the city, Red Cross workers directed them to the train station where they spent the night. The next morning, they boarded a special train reserved by the Arkansas National Guard to transport them to Little Rock.[104]

Mayor Overton caused a great deal of resentment when he asked Governor Carle E. Bailey of Arkansas to divert some of the refugees to high ground in his state in order to ease the congestion in the camps in Memphis. The *Forrest City Daily Times-Herald* ran the headline: "Memphis, The City Made Rich By Trade Of Persons In Flooded Areas, Does Not Want Refugees—Is Sending Them Out To Birmingham, Chattanooga, Jackson—Anywhere But There." The irate writer of an editorial quoted Bailey who said that Overton made a long-distance telephone call and "pleaded like a baby" for Arkansas National Guardsmen to turn refugees away from the Harahan Bridge. The newspaper's editor charged that Overton overstated the number of refugees in Memphis, especially the number of sick, in order to justify not taking any more refugees from Arkansas. The writer simply could not believe that fifty thousand refugees would head for Memphis and worried that relocated plantation workers would not return to eastern Arkansas.[105]

The disaster committee and the Red Cross faced the daunting task of caring for the sick after clearing all 9,200 people out of the fairgrounds. By January 31, local hospitals held more than 500 ill refugees while Central

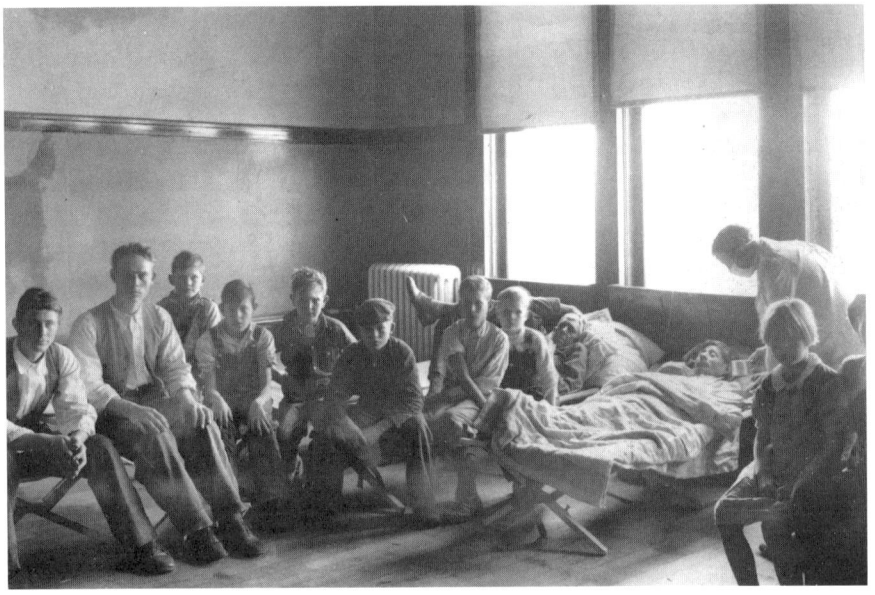

Mexican refugees from Hughes, Arkansas. *Courtesy of the Memphis and Shelby County Room, Memphis Public Library and Information Center.*

High School held 1,012, Lawler School had 143, the old Shelby County Hospital had 120 and Booker T. Washington High School had 681 patients. Fairview High School, next to the fairgrounds, took over 200 white refugees requiring nurses, while tuberculosis patients, both black and white, went to Oakville. Medical staff set up prenatal and postnatal clinics at Cummings School and conducted deliveries at Ella Oliver Home, which had 24 patients and 6 new babies by February 1. Workers built a temporary isolation ward on the John Gaston Hospital grounds and equipped Tech High School as an emergency hospital. Como House housed contagious patients, including a single family with fourteen cases of tuberculosis. Madison Heights School also took the contagious and the Shelby County Hospital on Mullins Station Road housed the elderly. In all, the disaster committee moved approximately 3,800 refugees from the fairgrounds to local city and county public schools.[106]

Not every member of a family required hospitalization, so health workers sometimes had to separate infants and small children from quarantined mothers to keep them from becoming ill. Georgia Tann of the Tennessee Children's Home Society placed them in temporary homes while their mothers recovered. The *Memphis Press Scimitar* appealed for volunteers to care for the youngsters, assuring readers that doctors had thoroughly examined

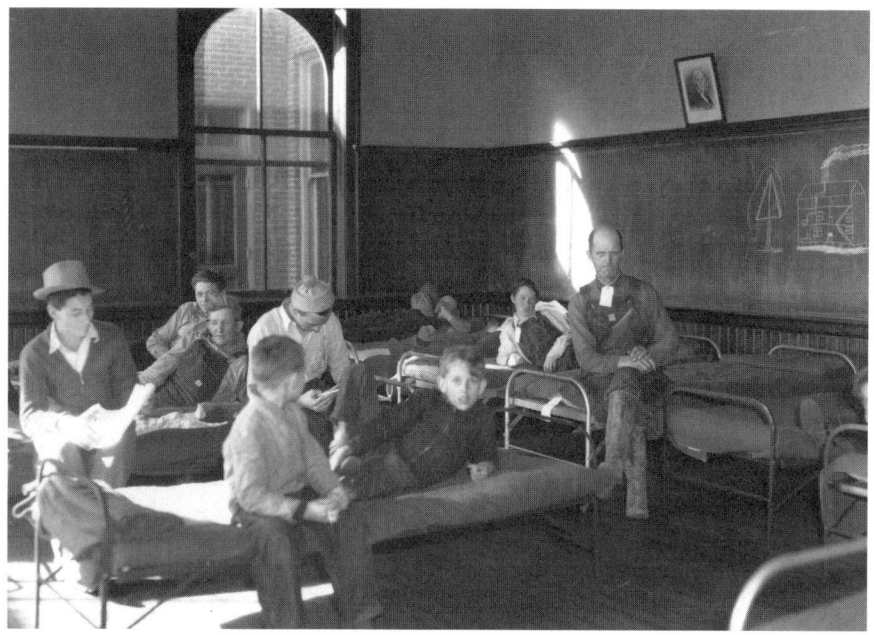

Refugees at Central High School wearing tags after processing and inoculations. *Courtesy of the Memphis and Shelby County Room, Memphis Public Library and Information Center.*

each child. Tann preferred foster parents who had adopted children through her agency in the past but allowed others to take in children after she determined their suitability.[107]

Meanwhile, a steady stream of Arkansans continued to flee to Memphis. The disaster committee soon found that relocating the refugees only made room for more. By February 3, the city had almost 28,000 registered refugees with more than 1,000 appearing daily. Additional relief supply offices opened around town because of the long lines at Ellis Auditorium. Overworked officials encouraged many of the newly arrived not to stay. W.I. Jones, Red Cross area director, urged out-of-town refugees to accept transportation to other camps farther east of town.[108]

Officials in Washington, D.C., once again became concerned about sanitation in the Memphis facilities. U.S. Army major general George Van Horn Moseley sent Lieutenant Colonel E.B. Maynard, Medical Corps surgeon of Fort Oglethorpe, Georgia, to inspect the refugee facilities in Memphis. He and Lieutenant Colonel Howell M. Estes, Sixth Cavalry, Fourth Corps Area representative, arrived on February 1 and met with Mayor Overton at 10:00 a.m. After the meeting, Maynard set up an office in the city courthouse along with the Mayor's Disaster Committee. He and Estes inspected the city's hospitals and found them well organized, well staffed and amply supplied although they lacked isolation units needed to contain the spread of serious diseases. As the inspections progressed, Maynard became increasingly concerned with the conditions in the refugee centers at the schools. Refugees received their shots but no one inoculated the personnel in direct contact with them, leaving workers at risk of infection. The health department and many of the school principals could not maintain discipline and sanitation in the overcrowded schools. The schools lacked adequate toilets, and many people relieved themselves on the floors and outdoors on the campgrounds. The schools had too few sinks, no places to bathe and staff placed the beds only a few inches apart, causing germs to spread easily between refugees during the night.[109]

Maynard made numerous recommendations to the mayor's flood committee, including reducing the numbers of refugees in each facility, assigning nurses and qualified city employees or veterans to enforce sanitation, vaccinating aid workers against typhoid and smallpox, thoroughly washing dishes, more frequent garbage removal, sweeping floors, making beds, having more trash cans available, ventilating the sleeping quarters at night and airing out mattresses twice a week outdoors. He also recommended a stricter hygiene routine for the refugees, including having everyone sleep head to foot, bathing at least twice a week, isolating anyone with a cold, not coughing or sneezing into the air, prohibiting spitting anywhere except into designated receptacles and not soiling the grounds in the concentration area.[110]

The following day, Dr. Lombard, head of the Public Health Service, worked in cooperation with the Red Cross to relieve the congested camps, continue the immunizations and improve sanitation. City health superintendent L.M. Graves and city sanitary engineer A.H. Fletcher returned to duty after having the flu to assist. Nearly fifty thousand refugees in 154 emergency centers of the Memphis area received immunization from smallpox and typhoid by this point. Lombard saw to it that medical personnel immunize emergency workers including those employed on levees and those patrolling the Mississippi River. As a further insurance against possible epidemic in refugee quarters, health authorities relieved crowded conditions by dividing the flood victims among the remaining unoccupied school buildings.[111]

Memphians held their breath as the flood crest reached Memphis on the night of February 9. When the levees held, the corps of engineers assured the relief officials they would not have to transfer the remaining refugees.

High Water Blues

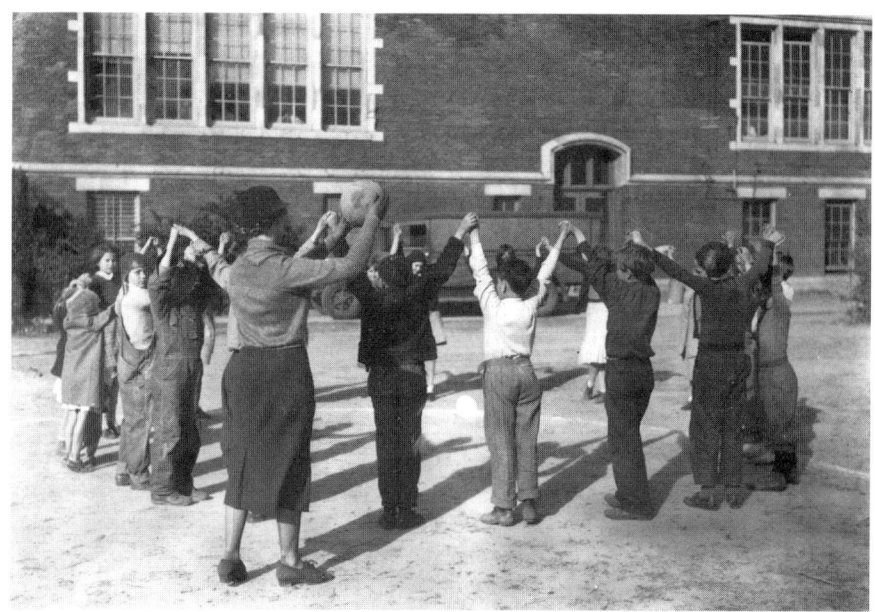

WPA worker playing games with refugee children at Fairview School. *Courtesy of the Memphis and Shelby County Room, Memphis Public Library and Information Center.*

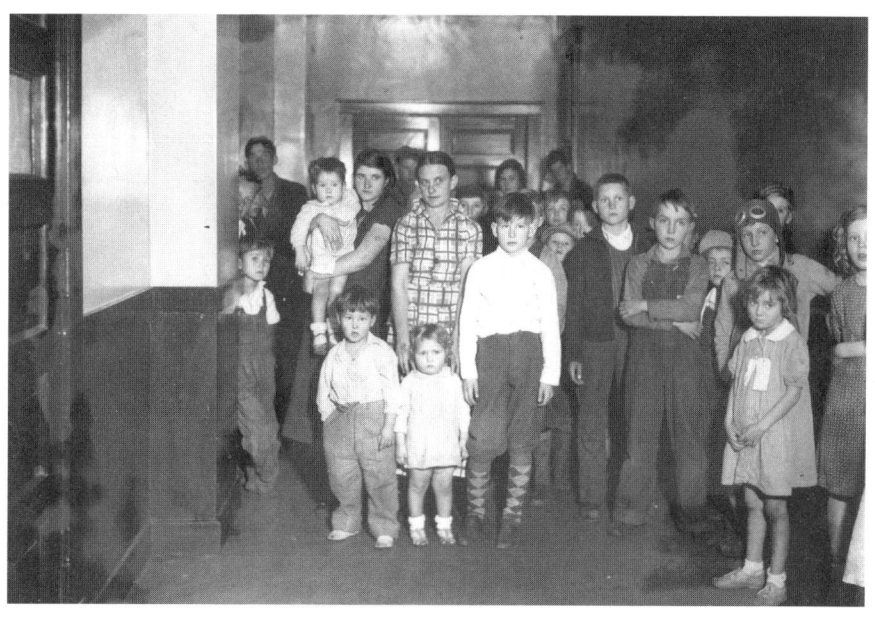

Refugee children at Fairview School, including some separated from parents. *Courtesy of the Memphis and Shelby County Room, Memphis Public Library and Information Center.*

The disaster committee then decided to move the remaining refugees out of most of the public schools. They relocated African American refugees to the Shelby County Hospital, which now had an adequate number of doctors, nurses, toilets, bathing facilities and a cafeteria to accommodate seven hundred people. White refugees returned to the newly renovated fairgrounds with improved toilets, bathing facilities and more recreation to improve morale. In addition, its proximity to the emergency hospital facilities at the Fairview School allowed family members to easily visit sick relatives.[112]

Memories of past outbreaks of disease, including yellow fever, made the disaster committee very aware of what could come of an uncontrolled epidemic. Even before the flood there was a national influenza problem and an unusually high rate of sickness across the United States. The United States had 23,258 new cases by January 22, about double the number of cases from the previous week. Hollywood film productions stopped because actors like Clark Gable became ill. During the months of January and February of 1937, influenza, pneumonia, bronchitis and upper-respiratory infections caused or contributed to the deaths of 330 residents and flood refugees in Memphis. The health department also reported 37 cases of tuberculosis, 2 cases of typhoid fever and 1 of diphtheria that resulted in deaths. City officials and local journalists publicly downplayed the severity of the situation and assured Memphians that health officials had taken every possible precaution to contain the spread of disease. This may have eased public anxiety to some degree, but the possibility of a widespread epidemic remained a genuine cause for concern for the disaster committee until the floodwater receded in March.[113]

FLOOD CAPITAL
OF THE NATION

Well, the rails are washed out north of town
We gotta head for higher ground
We can't come back 'till the water comes down
Five feet high and risin'
Johnny Cash, Five Feet High and Risin'[114]

President Roosevelt issued a proclamation on January 23 stating that the "disastrous floods in [the] Ohio and Mississippi River Valleys already have driven 270,000 from their homes." He predicted the number would increase until the floodwater crested and that snow, sleet and freezing weather added to the suffering and made more hazardous the work of the rescue. He understood that the flood victims relied on the American Red Cross for food, shelter, fuel, medical care and warm clothing and promised that various agencies of the federal government would cooperate with these efforts to the fullest extent.

Local governments and the Red Cross set up 1,575 refugee centers, often called tent cities, throughout the flooded areas with the help the U.S. Army and National Guard units to make refugees comfortable and restore some semblance of order to their lives. They also established supply warehouses in West Virginia, Ohio, Indiana, Arkansas and Tennessee, including Nashville, Knoxville and Memphis to collect materials for the refugees.[115]

In addition, Memphis once again became the center of rescue and relief operations for the flooded mid-South. The Red Cross and federal government

Memphis and the Superflood of 1937

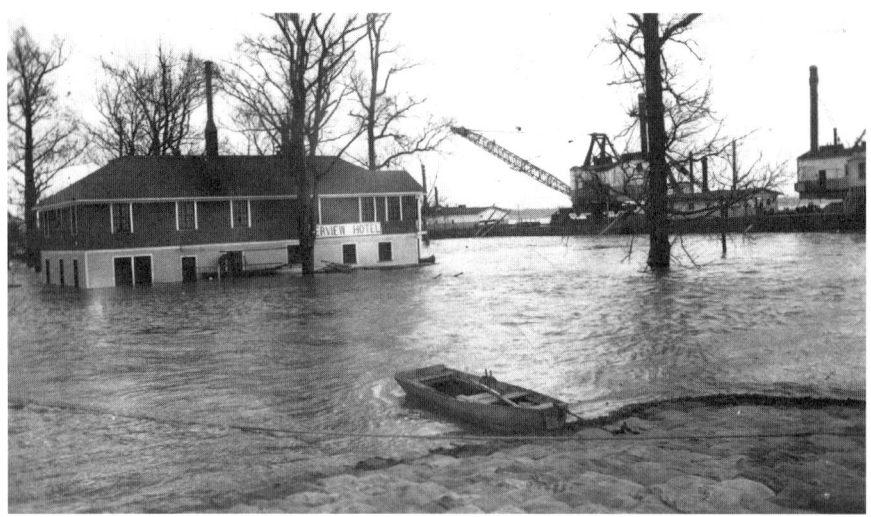

Riverview Hotel just outside the levee near West Memphis, Arkansas. *Courtesy of the Memphis and Shelby County Room, Memphis Public Library and Information Center.*

followed the general plans used during the Mississippi Valley Flood of 1927 and established a regional headquarters at Memphis. Soon, various government, military and relief officials set up operations in the city, followed by press agencies from around the country and the world. The city's position as a regional distribution center allowed various agencies to have access to river, road and air transportation. A huge fleet of naval and coast guard air and water vessels from around the country gathered to bolster rescue efforts. In addition to these services, Memphians raised money and volunteered to help refugees, all the while keeping a close watch on the ever-rising Mississippi River.

Red Cross chairman Admiral Cary T. Grayson issued a nationwide appeal on January 23. The endowment fund supplied by the organization's membership dues soon depleted, leaving a shortage of money for relief. Grayson asked the American public to donate $2 million, stating "the emergency is so great that no expense is spared to save lives and to protect these unfortunate victims of the rising waters." President Roosevelt, who also served as the president of the Red Cross, issued a proclamation in support of the fundraising drive. Grayson increased the quota to $5 million, and he increased it again to $10 million on January 26. Word spread through newspapers, radio, movie theaters, stage shows and benefits. After only three weeks, in the depths of the Great Depression, Americans raised $21 million to help to people of the Ohio and Mississippi Valleys.[116]

High Water Blues

The Memphis chapter of the Red Cross, headed by D. Eugene Wagner, quickly assembled to assist flood victims. Organized in 1917, the organization's members had experience with numerous disasters. The chapter officially formed after members provided assistance to troops who stopped at Union Station on their way south to engage Pancho Villa. The chapter also worked with soldiers returning from World War I through 1923. It re-formed in 1932 and provided aid to north Mississippi during the flood of 1935, the Shelby County community of Germantown during a flood in 1936 and Tupelo, Mississippi, following the devastating tornado of April 1936.[117]

The Red Cross began its fundraising and membership campaign in Memphis with broadcasts from WREC. Initial contributions arrived at the Red Cross office at Room 306, Empire Building and the *Commercial Appeal* newspaper offices. The newspaper had daily lists of contributors as an incentive for others to donate, and every person who gave a dollar or more received a Red Cross membership card. On January 28 alone, the *Commercial Appeal* received $3,479.53, including $350 from S.H. Kress & Company, $200 from the Memphis Country Club and $200 from S.W. Rubin of Pittsburgh, Pennsylvania, a visitor to Memphis. The Red Cross began its drive to raise $20,000. By the time the flood had passed, Memphians gave $75,616.02 as well as several freight cars full of clothing, food and other necessities.[118]

Granville Allison, a banker for the First National Bank in Memphis, kept track of the unusually large amounts of money coming to the Red Cross. The local chapter disbursed nearly half a million dollars in Shelby County alone. At one point, Allison had to send a check for $1 million to Nashville during the night. The check protector at the Red Cross office in the Sterick Building would not print a figure that high so Allison had to go to his bank. Once he arrived, the night watchman refused to let him in. Allison pleaded and argued, and the guard finally relented but insisted on standing by his side as he made out the check.[119]

Unfortunately, a few petty criminals profited from Memphians' generosity. Imposters took advantage of the fundraising drive by posing as Red Cross solicitors and taking donations intended for refugee assistance. Mary Poston, Red Cross executive secretary, began providing solicitors with proper credentials to present when asking for contributions after receiving complaints from residents in the Buntyn neighborhood.[120]

Numerous other organizations followed suit and held drives and staged events to collect money and other donations. Civic clubs, such as the Raleigh Garden Club, raised money to aid the Red Cross in feeding hungry refugees. Students at the University of Tennessee at Memphis gave a dance to raise funds for flood relief and a party was given at the Parkview Hotel as well. Local ministers made appeals on behalf of the Red Cross from their pulpits on January 31 with the goal to fill Red Cross coffers by Victory Day the following Wednesday. The chairman of the park commission, Joe Brennan, worked with the *Commercial Appeal* to organize a basketball game at the Gaston Community Center on January 30 between Ole Miss and Southwestern to raise money. The Red Cross reported that donations had topped $160,000 by January 30.[121]

Local theater and nightclub owners booked live performances and motion pictures to raise money for the Red Cross. Shows at the Orpheum, Warner Brothers and Colonel Cecil Vogel's Loew Theaters from January 27 to January 31 raised about $300 a night from their $0.50 admission. They featured performances from many local favorites who gladly donated their time to help raise money. The Orpheum Theater put on a stage show on the January 27 featuring the Orpheum Orchestra and performers from several roadshows stranded in Memphis followed by a full-length movie. The following night Claridge Hotel manager Lawrence Levy's Gray Gorden Orchestra and the entire Claridge floor show performed at the Orpheum. Other acts followed, including the dance team of Connie Rogers and Phil Finney, Nate Evans and his band, Smokey Land Man, Memphis Boy as a featured soloist, Mahon and Rucker dance team, Don Amoto and his human seal act, the Walker Trio and Gary Temple. The following Friday night Herman Waldman and his orchestra from the Peabody opened for Jimmy Joy and his band and the Claridge Floor Show. The Warner Brothers theater managers, Howard Waugh and Bill Hendricks, presented midnight showings of *Captain Blood*, and the Malco Palace show on January 30 began with a showing of *Trail of the Lonesome Pine* with Sylvia Sydney, Fred MacMurray and Henry Fonda. Following that were soloists Kay Gregory and Rex Pries with Herman Waldman's Orchestra, Nate Evans and Band, Joe Bisio, Helen Burfee, master of ceremonies Bill Fielding, Billy Middleton and slingshot expert Dan Dudlaw.[122]

Money soon came in from other countries as well. On February 2, President Roosevelt proclaimed an emergency and allowed duty-free foreign donations. Chinese finance minister H.H. Kung, with the consent of Generalissimo Chiang Kai-shek organized a group of leading citizens who started a nationwide fundraising campaign in China. By February 3, Filipinos raised $11,000 for American flood relief, and even the Metlakatia Indians of Ketchikan, Alaska, sent what money they could raise for the Red Cross.[123]

High Water Blues

On February 19, staff of the *Chicago Defender* delivered by airplane money raised by African Americans in the Chicago area, many of whom had relatives in the mid-South. Although ignored by white Memphians, an enthusiastic crowd of black Memphians arrived at the Memphis Municipal Airport to welcome reporter Dan Burley and famous pilot Colonel John C. Robinson. Robinson, only the second African American pilot to land at the airport, graduated from the Tuskegee Institute and became the head of the Ethiopian Air Force and a close friend and personal pilot of Emperor Haile Selassie during Ethiopia's war against fascist Italy.[124]

The Brown Condor gave a thirty-minute interview on radio station WNBR before being taken to a public reception at T.H. Hayes and Sons's undertaking parlor at 680 Lauderdale Street. The elite of the city's African American community showed up to greet the aviator. He met with park commissioner Lieutenant George W. Lee, businessman T.H. Hayes and L.J. Searcy, head of the Memphis Community Welfare League. Even the normally camera-shy Robert Church Jr. posed for a picture with Robinson and Burley at the airport before they returned to Chicago on March 12.[125]

National and international reporters rushed to Memphis to cover the developing flood in the mid-South. Ace special event announcers such as Dave Driscoll and Howard Barnes from WOR in Newark, New Jersey, arrived in Memphis to make the nationwide broadcasts from the five local radio stations. By the beginning of February, even the British Broadcasting Corporation had their American representative, Felix Greene, broadcasting from Memphis. People around the country and the world listened intently as these reporters relayed stories of human drama and devastation as the flood roared through the Mississippi Valley.[126]

Radio played an important role in not only allowing reporters to broadcast news to the world, but it proved invaluable in coordinating relief efforts. Reporters broadcast information to rescue workers and victims by the four large radio stations and smaller shortwave stations in the flood areas. On January 23, chairman of the Federal Communications Commission A.S. Prall authorized WMC managing director Henry W. Slavick to increase his station's broadcasting wattage from a thousand to fifteen thousand watts in order to broadcast nightly flood warnings and relief instructions. WMC also canceled regular programming and broadcast bulletins and weather information on a twenty-four hour schedule while WNBR and WHBQ continued regular programming with frequent updates. WREC canceled all regular programming and remained on-air continuously from January 24 through February 13 with flood reports and relief messages.[127]

Memphis and the Superflood of 1937

The Red Cross, U.S. Army, coast guard and other local, state and federal agencies established a communications network centered in Memphis to coordinate rescue operations that included radio, wire service, the air corps and messenger service. The coast guard, under Commander Henry Coyle, set up a radio center in the Red Cross headquarters, linking 240 stations and radio trucks at various locations, including Forrest Park. The corps of engineers had 23 radio stations, 21 river stations, and four hundred miles of field wire for 400 field telephones used by crews monitoring the levees.[128]

The Red Cross not only had to accommodate refugees arriving at camps, they also had to organize rescue missions to retrieve those stranded by floodwater. On January 27, Red Cross director George Myer took over rescue work from the corps of engineers. The engineers, who had shouldered the responsibility since the beginning of the flood, could now focus on saving weakening levees. The Red Cross coordinated with local organizations while teams traveled south from Cairo in advance of the flood crest warning residents to evacuate and transporting those stranded by rising water.[129]

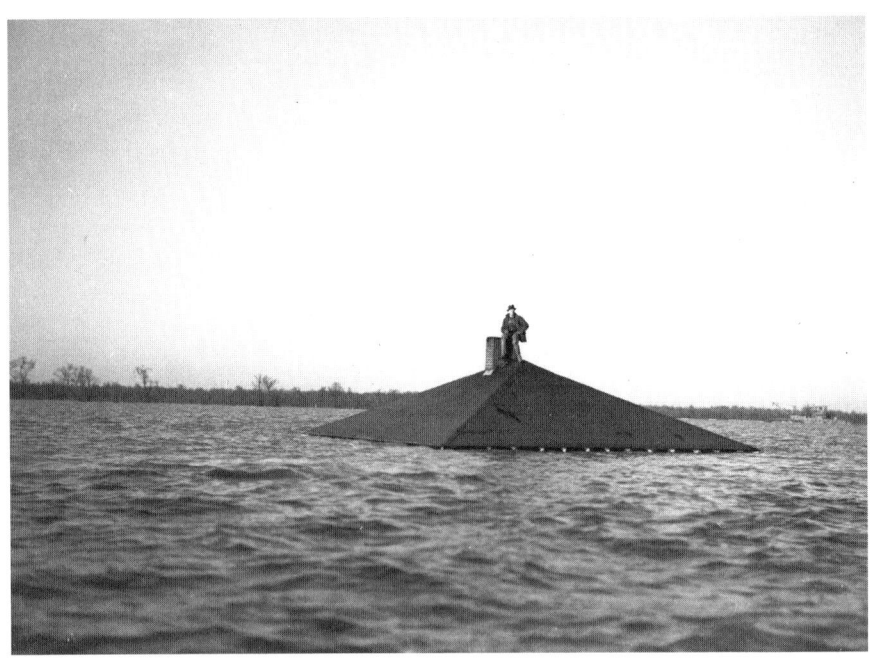

Refugee stranded on roof in eastern Arkansas. *Courtesy of the Memphis and Shelby County Room, Memphis Public Library and Information Center.*

High Water Blues

Rescue parties formed in communities from Tiptonville to Memphis to evacuate those already affected by the flooding and those who would need assistance if the new levees failed. H.G. Hurley of the Memphis district of the U.S. Army Corps of Engineers headed operations in Tiptonville where workers struggled with ice and fallen power lines to rescue flood victims. Thousands of highway patrolmen, National Guardsmen and volunteers struggled to keep levees intact before the corps of engineers finally advised those downstream in eastern Arkansas and west Tennessee to evacuate. Many refused to leave the rooftops of their houses or the tops of trees where they waited on hastily built platforms for the floodwater to subside.[130]

Memphians with access to watercraft rushed into Arkansas to transport people to safety while others used newly built boats. Crews at the board of education and Public Works Administration (PWA) workers, CCC men, army personnel, National Guardsmen and civilians supervised by the U.S. Army began building small outboard motorboats called johnboats to reach flood victims and transport materials. Crews in West Memphis and Vicksburg built additional johnboats—so many that they ran out of motors, forcing Reybold to authorize the purchase of sixty outboard motors from a factory in Waukegan, Illinois.[131]

On January 30, Tennessee Valley Authority (TVA) men from Wilson Dam, Norris, Chattanooga, Guntersville and Pickwick, under the command of Major Howard Ellis Davis, arrived to assist with rescue work. They set up a camp to accommodate 350 workers at Hodges Air Field on Jefferson Avenue near Somerville. It included tents with wooden floors, electric lights and iron cots as well as kitchens and medical facilities. They brought fifty light and twenty-five heavy trucks and shipped in by train flat-bottomed TVA boats capable of carrying 15 passengers.[132]

Since the state governors had not ordered evacuations, President Roosevelt ordered Major General H. Ford of the Ninth Army Corps to take charge of relief operations and move all residents in low-lying areas on the west side of the Mississippi River south of Cairo. Once the evacuation orders arrived, Myer placed all local rescue activities under the command of Lieutenant Colonel Douglass H. Gillette, of the corps of engineers, who also coordinated activities with liaison officers from the War and Navy Departments. The new czar of rescue worked closely with Dr. Louis Leroy, who had, up to that point, been in charge of rescue operations.[133]

Dr. Leroy remained active on the Mississippi River following the 1927 flood. He used his boating skills to help in rescue efforts when the Harahan Bridge caught fire in 1928; in 1929, he broke the record set in 1870 by the

Robert E. Lee in a race from New Orleans to St. Louis. During the 1937 flood, he spent five tense days and nights directing the Red Cross rescue division from Rosedale, Mississippi, to Cairo, Illinois, supervising the rescue flotilla. Leroy oversaw and conducted much of the rescue work along the Mississippi River while retired engineer William Parkin supervised rescue work on the tributaries.[134]

Under Leroy's direction, relief workers rescued over two thousand families from lowlands and islands, with much of the work done with the steamer *Joe Curtis*. On January 24, they evacuated two white families and fifty African American families from President's Island before the river completely covered it. Over the next three days, plantation owners Joe Sailors of Memphis and L.F. Etter of Marion, Arkansas, accompanied Leroy as he used the *Joe Curtis* to remove the tenant families, livestock, grain, household goods and farm equipment. Leroy helped rescue several families from Mhoon Landing and about forty more families from President's Island on February 1. The next day Leroy took the *Joe Curtis* to Thelma Landing, Arkansas, thirty miles south of Memphis to evacuate seventy-five more families.[135]

W.O. "Barney" Butler, who later worked as director of attendance and records for the board of education, recounted how typical rescue operations worked. He said "we'd go into flooded areas in small boats with outboards and get people and then take them out to barges on the river." Workers spent many hours cold, wet and tired. (One exhausted volunteer fell asleep on a barge during a break. After sleeping soundly, he awoke surprised to find that he had been sleeping with a pig.) Butler worked for two weeks in the same set of clothes, bringing in over nine hundred people from the backwoods and bottoms as far south as Greenville, Mississippi, and north almost to Cairo, Illinois. He and his co-workers rescued many refugees who cut holes in their roofs to climb to the tops of their houses to escape the floodwater.[136]

Thousands fled to Memphis but only about half of the population in the flood zones left before the water reached them. Red Cross director Myer believed many lowlanders drowned because they refused to evacuate until the water hit their doorsteps. Many family members stayed behind to guard against looters or save their livestock. Captain Joe Overall, who piloted the steamer *Charles D. Harris* in search of flood victims, encountered many who refused to leave their homes.

Fifty years later, Overall recalled:

> *People's houses would be floating out there in the flood. Cows, chickens, hogs and everything floating and, y'know, those people wouldn't get on and*

High Water Blues

go to higher ground: just hundreds of them. We had a terrible time getting those people out of that backwater. They wanted to stay with their cows and drown, and a lot of them did drown.[137]

By January 30, an enormous fleet of water vessels and aircraft gathered at Memphis, which the *Commercial Appeal* now called the flood capital of the nation. Red Cross officials boasted the greatest rescue fleet on either coastal or inland waters in preparation to meet the flood crest coming downriver. Over a thousand watercraft and thirty aircraft remained on standby between Cairo, Illinois, and Rosedale, Mississippi. The flotilla began with two picket boats from New Orleans, followed by six 165-foot, eight 125-foot and nine 75-foot patrol boats that acted as shelter and communication centers for the crews of smaller rescue boats. Soon, six coast guard vessels from Galveston, Texas, and a number of other boats ranging from 26 to 36 feet in length joined the operation. Investigators with the federal alcohol tax unit, who with the coast guard normally searched for moonshine stills, used their eleven boats and two amphibious airplanes to evacuate people and livestock from river islands between Memphis and Helena. Captain Reinberg, commander of all coast guard relief forces, joined Commander Coyle in Memphis after the flood crest passed from the Ohio River into the Mississippi River. He

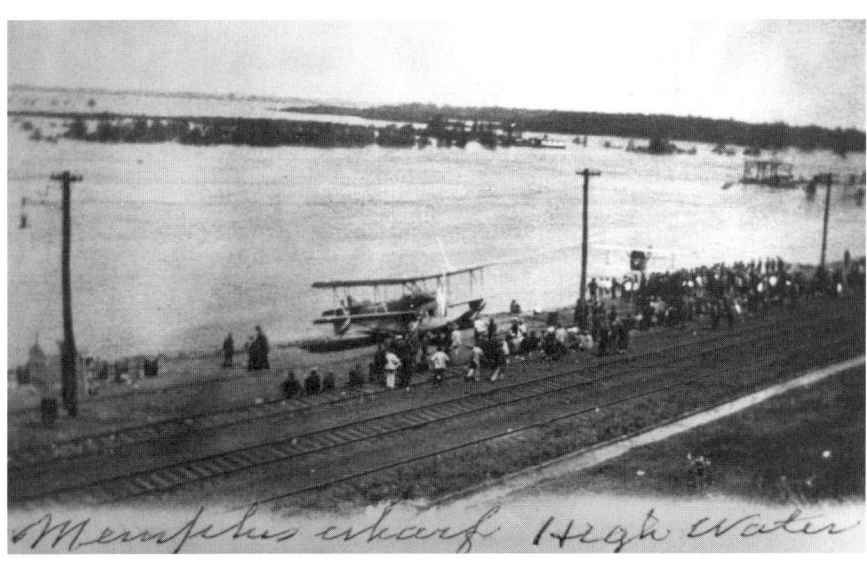

Crowds gather to see amphibious airplanes land at wharf. *Courtesy of the Memphis and Shelby County Room, Memphis Public Library and Information Center.*

brought more personnel that brought the number up to three hundred; additional boats, up to sixty-four; and six observation airplanes.[138]

Memphis not only had an enormous flotilla of water vessels, but it had an impressive fleet of aircraft as well. By February 1, Memphis Municipal Airport hosted the largest concentration of aircraft in its history. Airport officials now had to carefully coordinate the normally unrestricted Memphis area air traffic because of the congested skies. The hangars filled up quickly, forcing crews to stake down many airplanes outside, including the *Detroit News* flying studio. The blimp Resolute arrived to replace the Pure Oil Company's trimotor airplane as the means to photograph and chart the progress of the flood. Unlike the airplane the blimp had a radio and public address system to communicate with people on the ground.[139]

Rescue work even extended to parts of Memphis and Shelby County. On January 25, crews rescued from trees several people who had been trapped by the sudden flood of the area around the Nonconnah Creek. Knee-deep water surrounded some houses as water from the Wolf River reached Chelsea Avenue and backed up Cypress and Lick Creeks, and more than eight hundred telephones lost service because of frozen and broken lines.

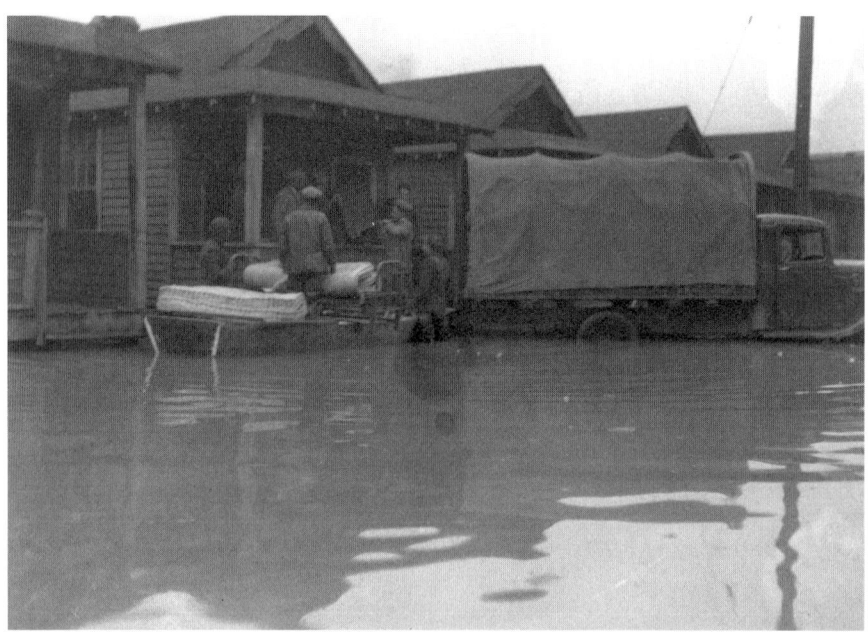

City crews arrive with trucks to evacuate residents of Sunflower Street in North Memphis. *Courtesy of the Memphis and Shelby County Room, Memphis Public Library and Information Center.*

High Water Blues

Many residents in North Memphis heeded warnings and moved out of their homes in anticipation of flooding. However, others stayed until workers had to use boats to rescue them. Removal director O.P. Williams oversaw the use of city equipment in the transportation of three or four families per day in North Memphis as their homes went underwater.[140]

Memphis experienced occasional flooding resulting from backwater overflowing from the Gayoso Bayou, the Wolf River, Nonconnah Creek and its tributaries. Floods in 1912, 1913 and 1927 caused damage in low-lying areas of the city and engineers responded by improving levees and pumping stations Memphians felt secure with the new flood control measures in addition to their position on high ground, but this new flood changed that. Stories in the press about the havoc caused along the Ohio River caused a great deal of anxiety in the mid-South. As the river stage reached record levels, many wondered if Memphis would suffer the same fate as cities in the Ohio Valley. It soon became clear that Memphians faced the twin tasks of both caring for thousands of refugees and saving their city from the flood.

SUPERFLOOD

The greatest flood threat in the history of the Mississippi Valley now exists...a super flood[sic] *is on the way.*
—Lieutenant Colonel Eugene Reybold, U.S. Army Corps of Engineers,
Memphis district, January 25, 1937[141]

Night approached and the rising river lapped at the base of the sea wall less than fifty feet away from Lieutenant Colonel Eugene Reybold's Memphis office. He could see a nearby steamer towing a barge with much-needed equipment and carpenters steadily building johnboats from his window. Inside, activity filled the office and his staff answered office telephones that constantly rang with calls from Vicksburg, Cairo and Washington. Reybold had prepared for a record flood but the latest reports, though vague, indicated that it would exceed all expectations. He called together various members of the Mayor's Disaster Committee, Red Cross, railroad officials and the Arkansas National Guard to give them the grim news of the latest flood forecast and begin preparations. He faced a difficult situation but his experience, leadership skills and vision made him the right man for the job.[142]

Reybold graduated from Delaware College in 1903 and was commissioned in the Coast Artillery Corps in 1908, where he was assigned to military housing and coast defense construction work. Stationed at Fort Monroe throughout World War I, he became commandant of the Coast Artillery School. He transferred to the U.S. Army Corps of Engineers in 1926 and served as district engineer in Buffalo, New York; Wilmington, North Carolina; and eventually Memphis, where he commanded the district covering the Mississippi and its tributaries from Cairo, Illinois, to the mouth of the Arkansas River. He would later receive an appointment as chief of engineers shortly before the Japanese attack on Pearl Harbor, directing the corps' tremendous range of activities throughout the war and becoming the first officer ever to rank as lieutenant general while chief of engineers. He credited his training at the Command and General Staff School and the War College with his ability to face the 1937 flood. He observed: "My military training and similar training of countless engineer officers sent to my assistance had a lot to do with the safe passage of the greatest flood the lower Mississippi Valley ever experienced."[143]

Reybold faced a room full of anxious officials in the impromptu gathering on January 25. Time was short so he cut to the chase. He called the meeting to order and announced: "The greatest flood threat in the history of the Mississippi Valley now exists…a super flood[*sic*] is on the way." He informed the conference members that—assuming the precipitation would stop—Memphians should expect a flood stage of 55 feet within twelve days. The stunned officials could hardly believe what they heard. The flood stage would exceed the flood of 1927 by 9.5 feet, far more than what any levee could withstand. Some refused to accept Reybold's prediction. They believed the Arkansas levees would give out before the Mississippi River reached 55 feet. Others argued the frozen earthen levees would hold, allowing the river to reach its full crest. Regardless, the city faced imminent danger. Even if the Arkansas levees collapsed and the crest only reached 50 feet, this still meant almost the entire area of Memphis between the Wolf River and Chelsea Avenue would flood as well as about half the area extending to Jackson Avenue.[144]

Everyone present at the meeting agreed with Reybold about sparing no expense or effort in fighting the flood. They followed the reports of the devastation caused by flooding in Paducah, Louisville and Cincinnati as well as the daily lists of drowning victims reported in the *Commercial Appeal*. Reybold did not know if the mainline levees would hold but planned to make every effort to prepare for the worst. He organized patrols of alphabet workers (WPA, CCC, NYA, etc.) to find low places in the levee and immediately mud box them (building a mud wall between a planked form) or sandbag them. Since the engineers could not order an immediate evacuation of property over which they did not have jurisdiction, they agreed to Reybold's recommendation that the governors of Missouri, Arkansas and any other state affected should prepare to declare martial law and evacuate residents if the mainline levees gave out. If the civil authorities ordered evacuations, army engineers recommended that the rule of the sea apply: women and children first. They would recruit all available men for levee work as done by officials in Cairo, Illinois. No one really knew what to expect other than a flood crest worse than any before, and fortifying the levees could only go so far in containing the river. The situation had become desperate, but the new flood control measures had one more contingency: one that ironically required the deliberate destruction of thousands of acres of farmland.[145]

The corps of engineers had a backup in the event a Mississippi flood stage ever surpassed sixty feet. Under an act of Congress, the corps purchased flowage rights through a 130,000-acre strip of rich plantation land extending from Bird's Point to New Madrid, Missouri, to divert excess floodwater. The engineers designed the $21 million low-level "fuseplug" levee across the face of the spillway to collapse once the river reached a certain level. The water would then flow down between the riverfront levee on the Missouri shore and a setback levee located about five miles to the west. The water would return to the Lower Mississippi just above New Madrid, where the volume of the flow would not pose a threat to the integrity of the mainline levee system. The corps allowed farmers to cultivate the land in the spillway as long as they understood the corps would flood the area if necessary to save Cairo. Naturally, property owners, tenant farmers and sharecroppers who lived in the area hoped the government would never issue a warning to evacuate but, with the floodwater lapping at the top of the Cairo sea wall, they knew time had run out.[146]

Reybold had prepared for this possibility. Under the advice of the Mississippi River Commission, he ordered the farmers in the floodway to evacuate on the afternoon of January 21. WMC and WREC agreed to broadcast a notice to leave while crews printed and distributed hundreds of handbills giving notice of the evacuation. Reybold sent a radiogram to his civilian assistant W.A. Steel at Cairo at 1:50 p.m. on January 24, ordering him to open the Bird's Point–New Madrid Floodway. The engineers designed the fuseplug just south of Cairo Point to collapse when floodwater reached 57 feet, but the frozen ground still stood firm. With the gauge at an all-time high of 57.5 feet at Cairo, Reybold ordered Major Roy Burdick and his engineers to either cut a trench into the retaining wall or blast it with dynamite. They hoped that flooding the 131,000 acres stretching along the west side of the Mississippi River to New Madrid, Missouri, would drop the water level 1 to 2 feet at Cairo.[147]

MEMPHIS AND THE SUPERFLOOD OF 1937

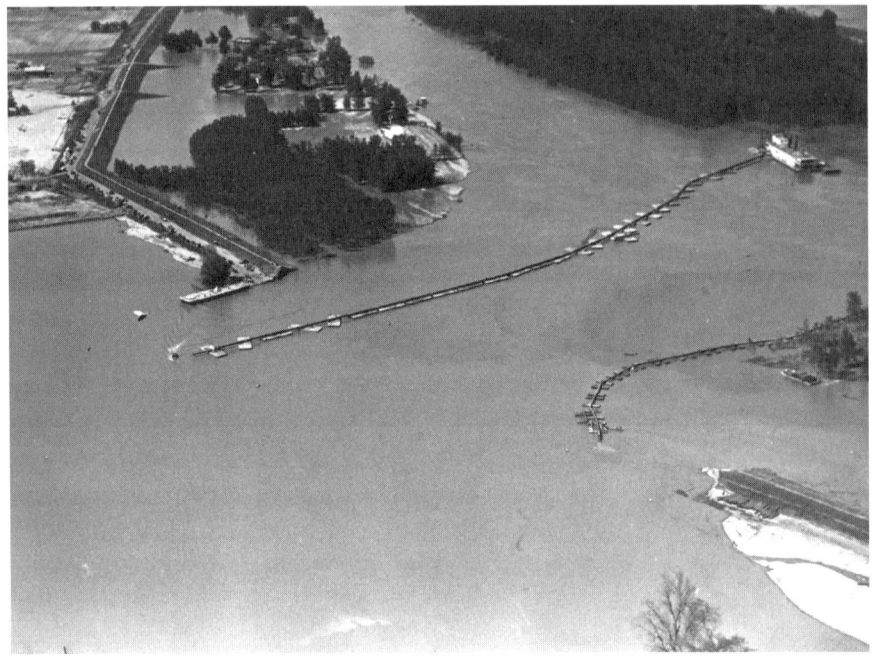

Flooded area of the Bird's Point–New Madrid Floodway. *Courtesy of the University of Memphis Special Collections.*

Some farmers refused to give up the land despite their agreements with the government. A number of armed farmers went so far as to hold Burdick and his team at bay as they approached the levee that afternoon in order to keep them from blasting. Burdick retreated until the following morning at 6:45 a.m. when Company K of the Missouri National Guard, under orders from Governor Stark, provided an armed escort to the sight. This time the farmers retreated, allowing the engineers to begin blasting. *Commercial Appeal* correspondent Jack Lockhart watched from the federal barge line boat *Tom Sawyer* as the Bird's Point fuseplug levee was blown in four places. He reported that engineers made two cuts just across the river from Cairo and two more four or five miles downriver. The explosions sent barrel-sized masses of mud a quarter of a mile away but the frozen ground would not give way. Dynamiting continued the next day by explosives expert Priestly H. Williams of the Austin Powder Company of Memphis. The fuseplug finally collapsed after twenty-one blasts created a three-thousand-foot opening.[148]

The Bird's Point–New Madrid Floodway quickly became a very dangerous place. As sleet fell, a steady flow of people evacuated the floodway with most taking only what they could carry on their backs since the spillway filled at a rate of about two inches per hour. Most farmers herded cattle off for slaughter but others simply left their stock to drown. Soon the water in many places became too deep for vehicles or to travel by foot. Even so, many still refused to leave. Rescue workers eventually had to use boats to evacuate diehards. Not everyone got out of the floodway in time despite the rescue efforts; three people drowned and officials reported at least four others missing. Pilots had a difficult time navigating because of the unpredictable waters. The worst accident occurred when a barge with over a hundred WPA workers sank several miles south of Prairie, Missouri.[149]

To make matters worse, opening the floodway had no immediate effect. The river at Cairo only fell from 58.6 feet on the afternoon of January 25 to 57.9 feet on the morning of January 28. At this point it was not clear whether opening the fuseplug or any part of the new flood-control measures would make a difference. Congressman William Madison Whittington of the Third Mississippi District, Representative Walter Sillers of Rosedale, Mississippi, and others characterized the Mississippi River and Tributaries Project as a monumental blunder. Reybold countered with his twice-daily press bulletins appearing in the local newspapers beginning January 23. He confidently assured mid-southerners that the Mississippi Valley could handle the flood crest and that the diverted floodwater into the Bird's Point–New Madrid Floodway would have a positive effect. On January 27, Reybold said "No crest waters have entered the district. No levee anywhere is in dangerous condition." Four days later, he wrote: "We are about to face the greatest flood crisis in the history of the Mississippi Valley…we face the test with confidence." He probably helped quiet some doubts, but the public remained understandably nervous. At 4:00 that afternoon, the Mississippi River reached a record height of 45.2, surpassing the flood crest of the flood of 1913.[150]

Reybold, Mayor Overton and the Red Cross not only had to reassure mid-southerners the levees would hold and Memphis could handle the refugees but they also had to convince officials in Washington as well. Not satisfied with written reports, Roosevelt sent WPA director Harry Hopkins and Major General Edward Murphy Markham to personally inspect operations in Memphis. On Friday, January 29, Hopkins and Markham, along with Surgeon General Dr. Thomas Parran; James Feiser, vice chairman of the National Red Cross; Lieutenant Colonel Francis C. Harrington, assistant WPA director; and Captain James C. Marshall, of the U.S. Army Corps of Engineers, traveled to Knoxville where they boarded the train the Memphis

Special for the two-day trip across the state. Hopkins told reporters from the back of his Pullman car: "We want to be damn sure the job [in Memphis] is met. We realize that this is the most serious flood in terms of the number of people involved that the nation has ever had. We intend to take nothing for granted." Even so, Hopkins and Markham did not want to give the impression any problems might exist. They publicly expressed confidence in Reybold's work in maintaining the mainline levees between Memphis and Cairo. Markham said "The pessimists who think otherwise can flow down the river with the rest of the debris."[151]

Hopkins and his party arrived in Memphis on February 1 and checked into the Peabody Hotel before setting out to see the flood firsthand. They boarded the flagship of the corps of engineers's fleet, the steamer *Inspector*, to examine the levee works north of Memphis. They returned the following morning and met with local officials including Mayor Overton, Colonel Waring and Commissioner Davis. Hopkins and his group left to inspect the refugee camps at Forrest City, Arkansas, and the U.S. Army Corps of Engineers's headquarters in West Memphis, Arkansas. Satisfied with what they saw, they returned to Memphis.[152]

Meanwhile, hundreds of workers bolstered levees around the city. Workers along the Nonconnah Creek reinforced the levee by building parallel boarded fences along the top to create an eight- to ten-foot trench they later filled with

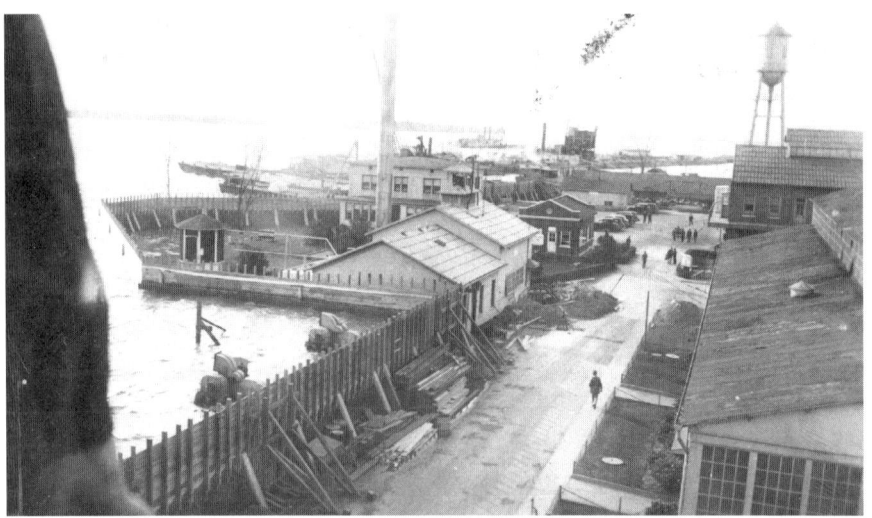

U.S. Army Corps of Engineers's office in West Memphis. *Courtesy of the Memphis and Shelby County Room, Memphis Public Library and Information Center.*

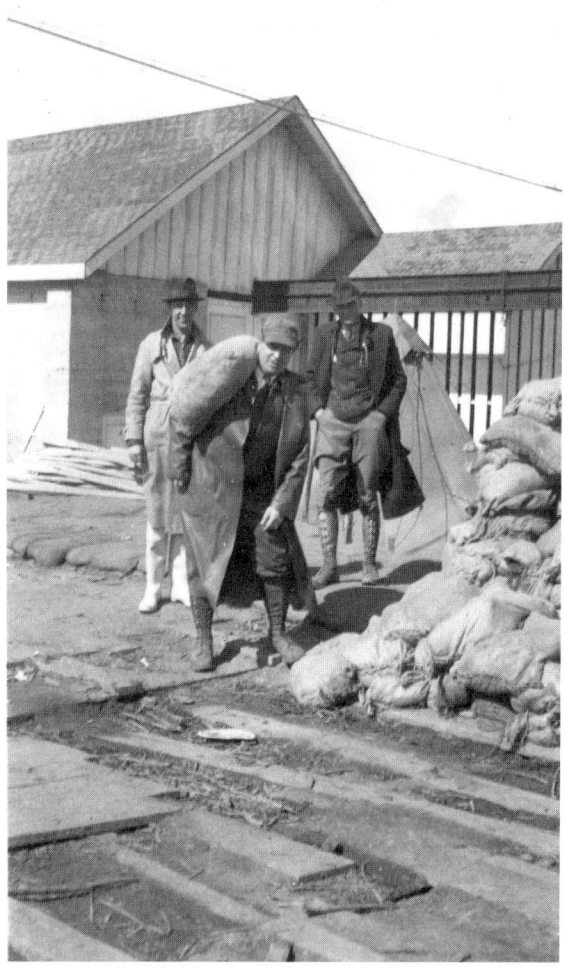

Levee workers carrying sandbags. *Courtesy of the Memphis and Shelby County Room, Memphis Public Library and Information Center.*

dirt to support an enormous wall of sandbags. Others along the downtown waterfront used sandbags and twenty-five thousand cotton bales, valued at nearly sixty dollars a piece, to build up the levee along Front Street.[153]

After dinner with the mayor, Hopkins visited the refugee centers and the local preparations for the flood fight. The inspections reassured Hopkins, who now said "the job was being met." Markham told reporters that the levees would hold barring heavy winds and rain. The next day Hopkins and his group continued up the river followed by an entourage of reporters.[154]

Dean Richard M. Gummerie, of Harvard University, happened to visit Memphis during the flood and observed relief efforts and levee work. What he saw greatly impressed him as he toured the flooded areas after attending a business meeting.

He said:

> *The sight of this city organized to face disaster makes an American glow with national pride. The quiet efficiency with which the Red Cross, Army Engineers, National Guard, and the City of Memphis are working in this crisis is as superb a demonstration of a nation's organizing genius as can be witnessed in today's world. It rivals even the rampant power of the Mississippi.*[155]

By January 16, the Mississippi River exceeded 3,500 feet in width at Memphis as it spread over the Arkansas lowlands toward the levees, and, by January 23, 14.02 inches of rain had fallen, breaking the previous record set in 1882. The flood stage reached 34 feet at noon on January 19. Water covered more than half of Mud Island (also known as City Island) and by the end of the week it was completely submerged. Memphis district engineers forecast a flood crest of 40 feet, upgraded it to 42 feet and then finally announced "with general rains forecast, the [flood] crest could not be predicted."[156]

The weather service had other problems in predicting the flood crest. Memphis had two different scales available to measure water depth that differed by almost three feet, and the newspapers had to report both since no one could agree on which one to use. They also received two sets of expert predictions. Memphis meteorologist F.W. Brist predicted a crest of 48 feet rather than 55 feet as Reybold predicted. Reybold then revised his crest prediction after conferring with district engineers at Cincinnati and St. Louis, General Harley B. Fergusson's office in Vicksburg and General Markham's office in Washington. Between January 25 and January 28, he came up with a figure of 53.6 feet, placing the Memphis district in the high-danger zone. That still did not satisfy Brist; he and Reybold continued to publicly disagree over flood-stage predictions until the flood finally passed two weeks later.[157]

On January 24, Reybold distributed another memorandum stating the peak river discharge at Cairo would reach 2.5 million cubic feet per second and could possibly produce a stage as high as sixty-one feet. He announced that "drastic efforts would be required if the area was to be saved; monetary considerations would not be a factor, and normal procedures in securing manpower and supplies were to be forgotten." Reybold turned the flood fight on the St. Francis River over to local officials and ordered all district personnel to return to Memphis to bolster the levees. The weather service could not reliably predict the coming flood stage so he ordered crews to prepare for the worst and "sack up" the levees for a possible fifty-five-foot flood stage.[158]

City engineers put pumping stations into operation and closed the four 6-foot cast-steel levee gates at the foot of Saffarans Street. Roy Johnson, North Memphis Pumping Station operator, switched on the four large drainage pumps to periodically empty reservoir water from the 2,130-acre Gayoso Bayou into the Mississippi River and used two additional pumps to remove sewage. Johnson never had to switch his pumps on at full capacity—not even during the 1927 flood. Even so, he took no chances. He remained at the pumping station day and night until the flood crest passed.[159]

Floodwater posed a danger to many residential and commercial sections in the northern and southern areas of Memphis because they sat in low-lying areas near rivers without adequate levees, floodgates or pumping stations.

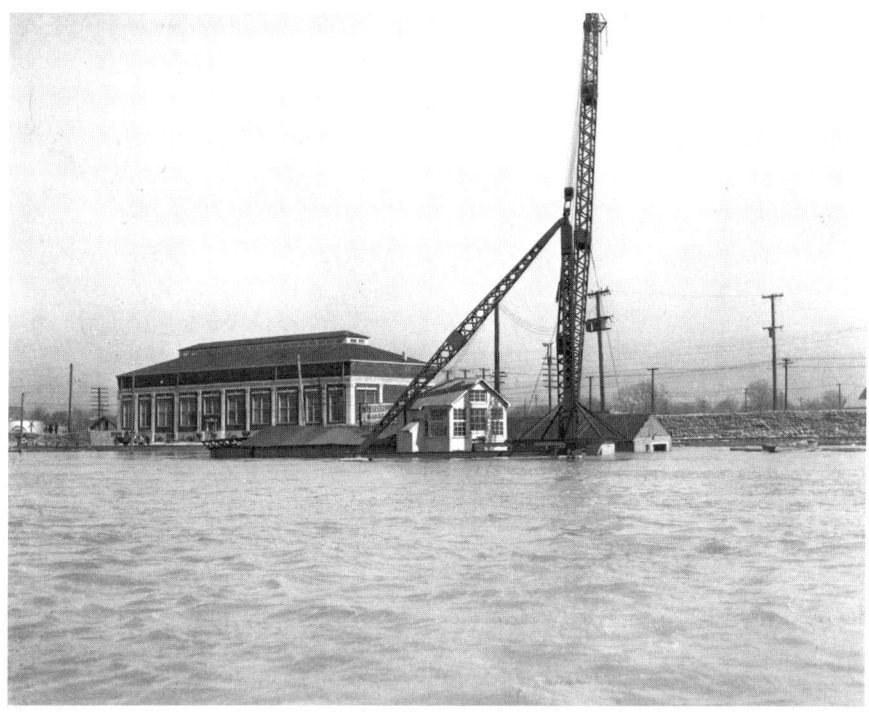

Floodwater from the Wolf River reaches the North Memphis Pumping Station. *Courtesy of the Memphis and Shelby County Room, Memphis Public Library and Information Center.*

Memphis and the Superflood of 1937

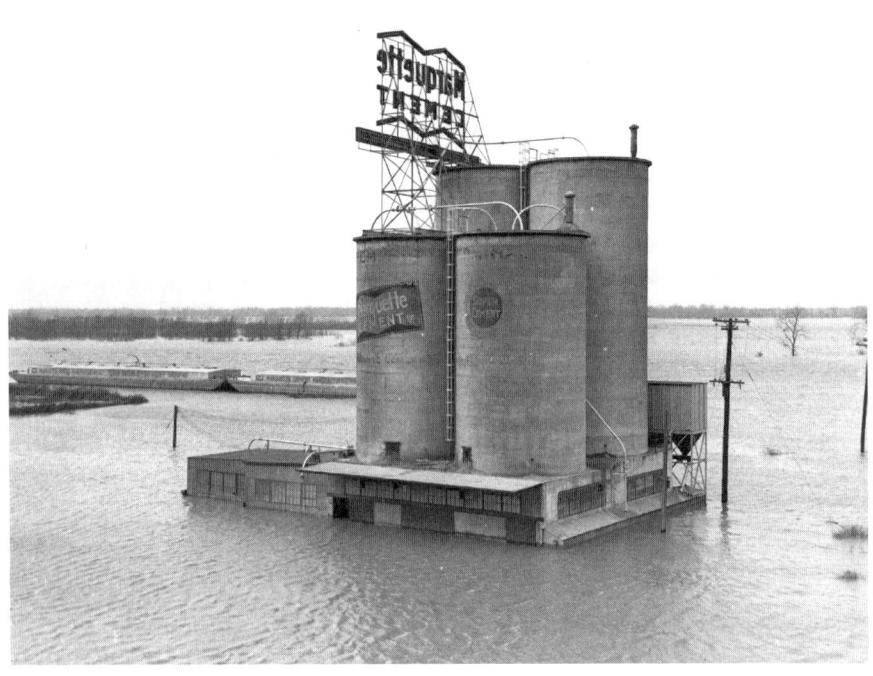

Floodwater surrounds the Marquette Cement Company. *Courtesy of the Memphis and Shelby County Room, Memphis Public Library and Information Center.*

Normally, the Wolf River and Nonconnah Creek and their tributaries flowed into the Mississippi but the high water of the Mississippi caused the opposite to happen. Now the water from the Mississippi flowed up the tributaries and spilled over, causing flooding in populated areas. Backwater from the Wolf River made its way into Cypress Creek, carrying it almost to North Parkway, while levees in the south weakened, allowing damage to the Federal Compress and Warehouse Company and other businesses.

Rain and backwater took a heavy toll on Memphis and Shelby County in the last weeks of January. Crews brought in truckloads of dirt from Woodstock, Tennessee, to bolster the caving banks on the approaches to the Thomas Street Bridge. Police, in the meantime, diverted traffic to the Payne Street Bridge in North Memphis. On January 21, police closed traffic on Riverside Drive between Beale and Georgia Streets, the drive between Wisconsin and West Trigg and Bon Air Street, south of Broad, where floodwater washed out a bridge. Lieutenant Toll E. Fowler of the Memphis Police Traffic Department closed Front Street between Washington and

High Water Blues

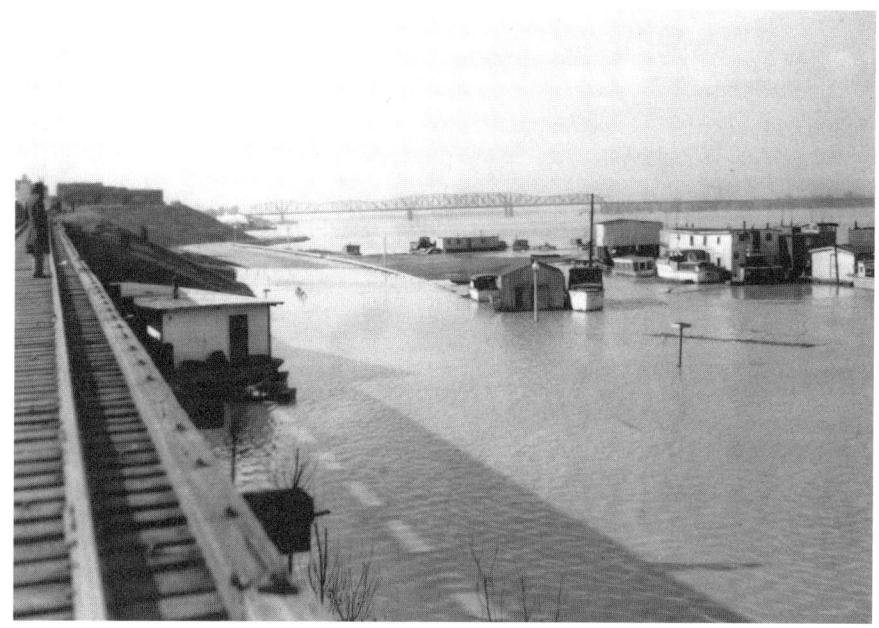

The Mississippi River spills over Beale and Riverside Drive. *Courtesy of the Memphis and Shelby County Room, Memphis Public Library and Information Center.*

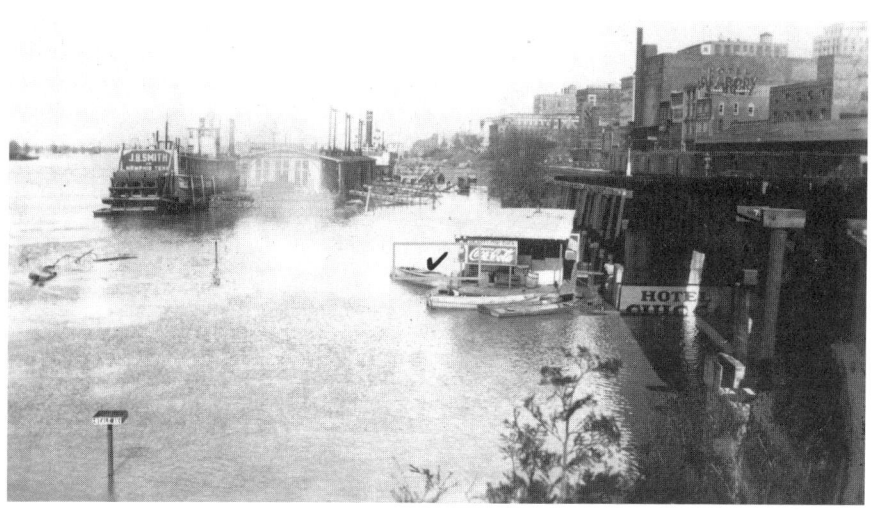

Floodwater covers Riverside Drive and Beale in downtown Memphis. *Courtesy of the Memphis and Shelby County Room, Memphis Public Library and Information Center.*

Memphis and the Superflood of 1937

Georgia while police and twenty-five National Guardsmen kept the curious from getting too close to the levees along the Wolf River, Nonconnah Creek and Riverside Drive to watch the rising water.[160]

All Shelby County roads near drainage ditches and rivers flooded, including Horn Lake Road that lead into Mississippi, Raleigh-Brunswick Road to Rosemark and Bolton College, Raleigh-LaGrange Road over Fletcher Creek and Houston Levee Road near Rosemark. The sheriff's department closed Houston Levee Road due to backwater from the Wolf River and closed Covington Pike because of overflow from Hatchie Bottoms. Before long, floodwater covered the principal north and west highways out of Memphis, limiting transportation to and from the city.[161]

Memphians also had to deal with ice and mud. On January 22, temperatures dropped twenty-three degrees and the rain turned to sleet. Ice damaged streets and power lines in the Chickasaw Gardens and Buntyn Station neighborhoods. WPA workers spread cinder on overpasses and intersections to keep traffic moving, and the Memphis Street Railway Company equipped trolleys with ice cutters and kept the service going

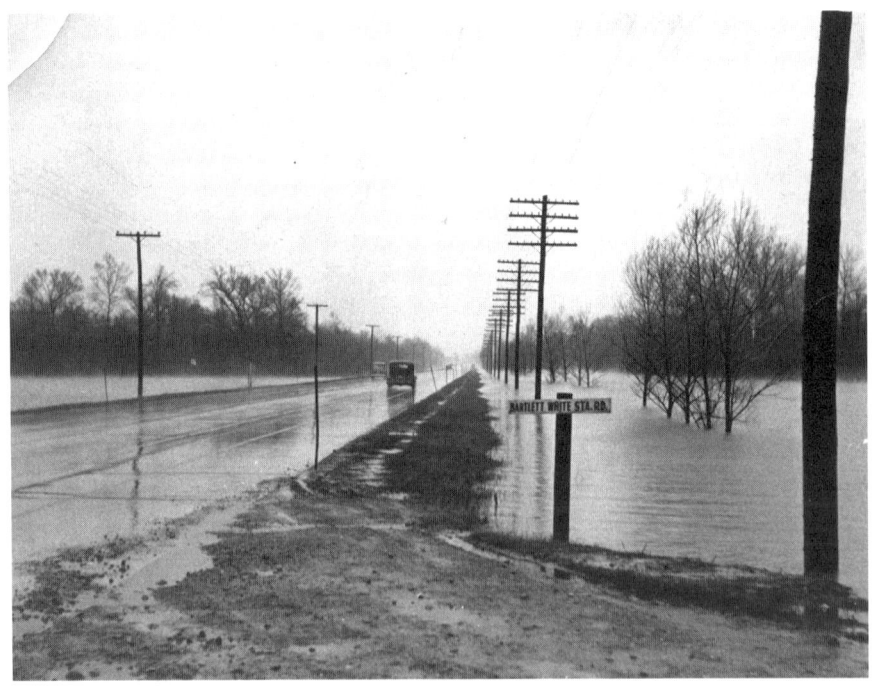

Flooding in Shelby County. *Courtesy of the University of Memphis Special Collections.*

High Water Blues

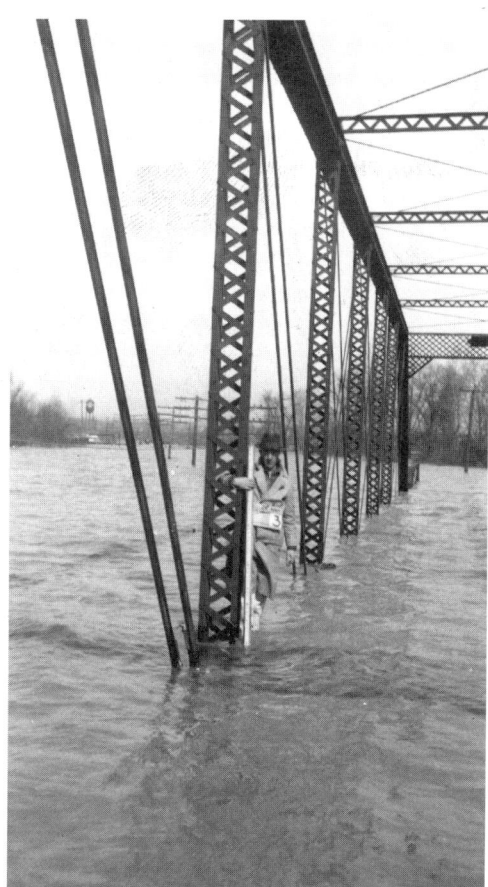

Right: The Wolf River washes out a bridge. *Courtesy of the Memphis and Shelby County Room, Memphis Public Library and Information Center.*

Below: Floodwater covers the IC Freight line at Peres in North Memphis. *Courtesy of the Memphis and Shelby County Room, Memphis Public Library and Information Center.*

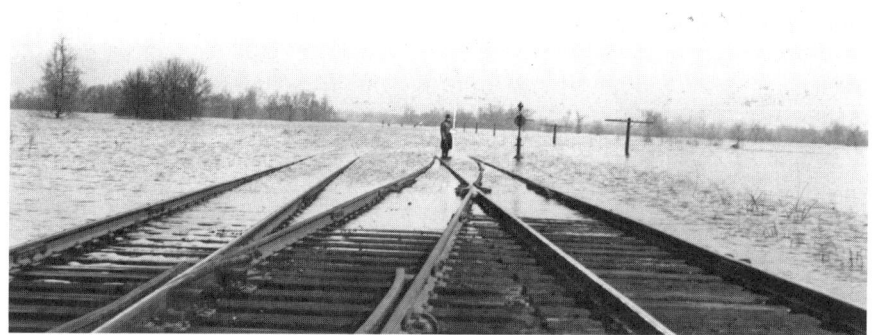

Memphis and the Superflood of 1937

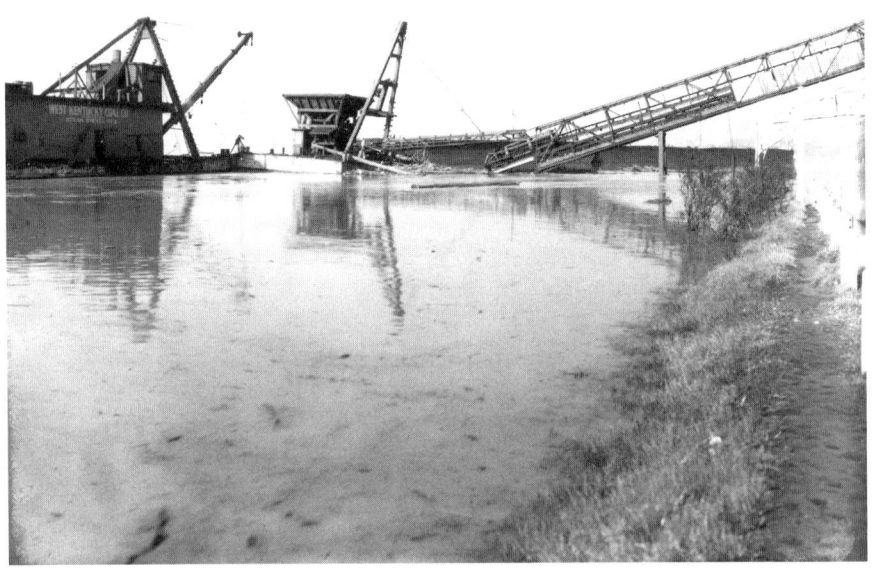

Floodwater threatens the West Kentucky Coal Company. *Courtesy of the Memphis and Shelby County Room, Memphis Public Library and Information Center.*

through the night in order to keep the lines free of ice. Mudslides slowed traffic on Benjestown Road and forced police to close Riverside Drive near the West Kentucky Coal Company. Another mudslide, one hundred feet wide and twenty feet deep, buried the Rock Island Railroad track near the Harahan Bridge, forcing railroad engineers to either stop or reroute trains.[162]

The Mississippi River reached a width of 3.25 miles at Memphis at 1:00 a.m. on February 3, resulting in extensive flooding in North Memphis. In light of what happened to cities in the Ohio Valley, local officials worried about possible fire and sewage problems. Backwater reached Jackson Avenue at Bellevue and the end of Carpenter Street in the Douglass neighborhood. The Cypress Creek backed almost to Vollintine Avenue; water from Lick Creek stood in Jackson Avenue at Montgomery and Olympic Streets; and drains as far south as the Madison Heights neighborhood spewed river water. Commissioner Davis and state fire marshals ordered gasoline tanks emptied and filled with water, and the Memphis Power & Light Company turned off gas in flood zones to avoid fire hazards.[163]

High Water Blues

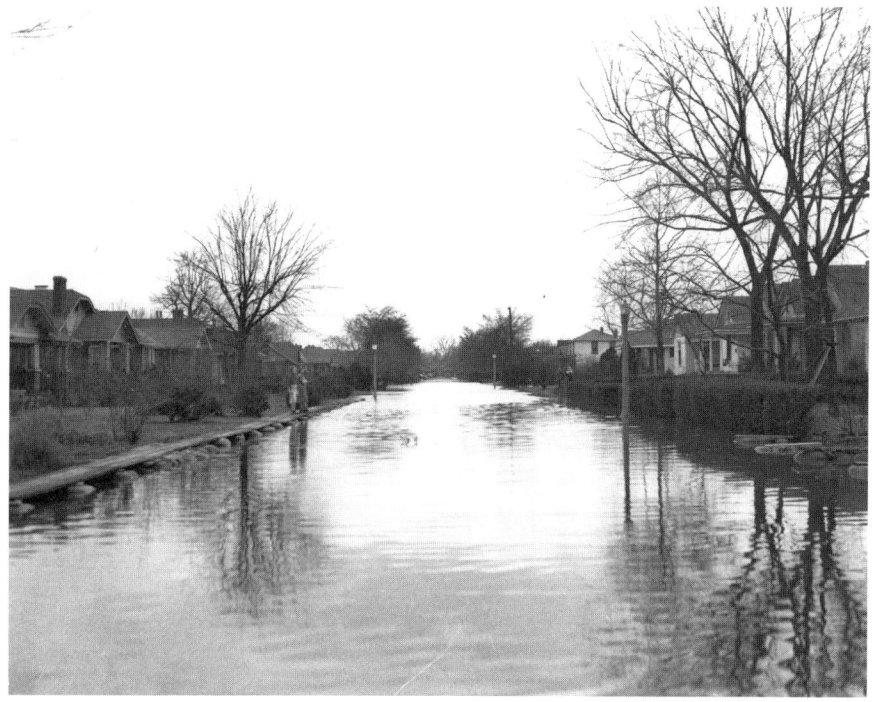

A flooded street in North Memphis. *Courtesy of the Memphis and Shelby County Room, Memphis Public Library and Information Center.*

The backwater became such a problem that evacuations eventually became mandatory. Public works set aside thirteen city trucks to move families out of flooded homes. The city received up to seventy calls a day to help move people out of North Memphis and, by the beginning of February, city crews moved more than five hundred people. Evacuations had been voluntary up to this point but, as the situation worsened, the health department received authorization to order people to leave their homes. On February 7, Mayor Overton issued the following statement:

> *The city of Memphis is using every precaution to protect the lives, safety and health of our citizens. Our levees are in splendid shape but it is humanly impossible to check backwater in certain outlying districts. In these districts we have to use precautions to protect health and to prevent fires. The health department has authority to evacuate where proper sanitation no longer exists. We ask the cooperation of the public, as every step we take is for the health and safety of the families affected by the high water.*[164]

Memphis and the Superflood of 1937

Overton met the rapidly appearing challenges of the flood without trepidation. He and his disaster committee worked well with state and federal agencies in making accommodations for the refugees, protecting the city from floodwater and calming anxious Memphians concerned over rumors of epidemics, food shortages and power outages. However, the need to make immediate decisions to meet a rapidly developing crisis led to friction within the political machine, and the mayor soon found his authority usurped by his most important benefactor. If Overton had any misconceptions about who really ran Memphis, Boss Crump soon cleared them up.[165]

BOSS RULE

Oh, the river's up and cotton's down,
Mister Ed Crump, he runs this town.
—*Artist unknown, Memphis fairgrounds, 1937*[166]

A number of businessmen, unhappy at the apparent lack of attention they received so far from the mayor, approached Ed Crump about saving their properties from the flood. Most saw Crump as the real power in Memphis anyway since he controlled all city and county elective offices and his political machine remained nearly undefeated in over sixty city and state elections. A *Time* magazine reporter wrote: "Edward Hull Crump has bossed Memphis so long that many Memphians hardly know they are being bossed. 'See Mr. Crump about it,' is a Memphis byword."[167]

Not surprisingly, many bypassed official channels and went straight to Crump in times of need. Crump may have left the flood crisis to Overton and the others if not for a telegraph received at his home late in the evening on January 29.

A number of fellow businessmen with shared interests in the South Memphis Land Company wrote:

> *The situation surrounding the big industrial section in new South Memphis is desperate. The water is creeping into our plants and we need help quick. The levee must be built up at once in order to protect the many million dollars invested. The Illinois Central Track should be taken up and the*

MEMPHIS AND THE SUPERFLOOD OF 1937

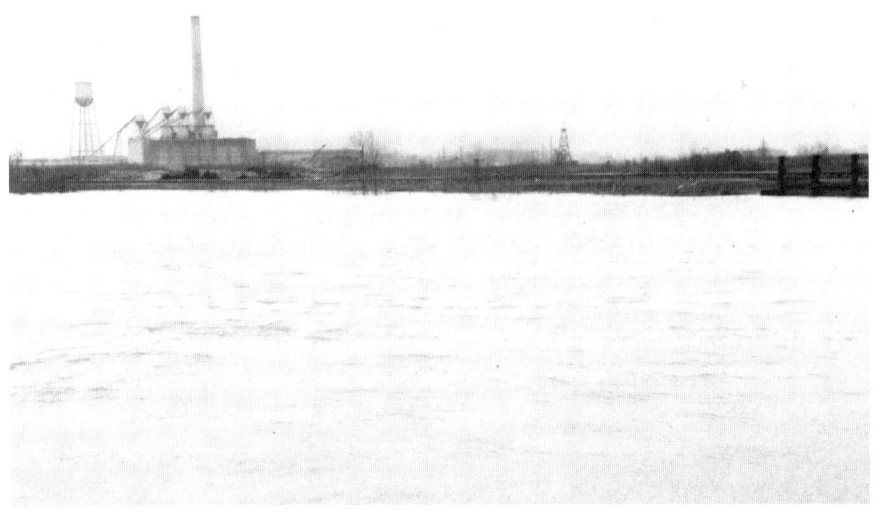

Floodwater approaching the newly opened Firestone Tire and Rubber Company. *Courtesy of the Memphis and Shelby County Room, Memphis Public Library and Information Center.*

dump properly sandbagged if this big manufacturing section is to be saved. May we have your cooperation and the help of the city and county authorities at once? The cooperation and facilities of the undersigned are at your disposal. This telegram is sent by the following concerns who are now at the Peabody [Hotel] *and are meeting with Mr. Hale tomorrow morning at 9:30 at the Memphis Compress and Storage Company Florida Street.*[168]

Crump returned to Memphis from New Orleans a week earlier with a cold that kept him on "the sick list." Crump would have normally taken a leadership role in any sort of crisis but, instead, he left the day-to-day operations to Mayor Overton while he recovered from his illness. He missed the initial formation of the Mayor's Disaster Committee and its cooperative efforts with the Red Cross, U.S. Army Corps of Engineers and other agencies. He could only keep up with events through occasional telephone calls and written correspondence, which proved very limited in a situation where circumstances changed by the hour. This new telegram left Crump with the impression that Overton could not keep pace with the emergency. He now felt compelled to personally take charge even at the expense of usurping Overton's authority, marking the first time Crump seriously questioned Overton's abilities.[169]

High Water Blues

After the meeting at the Memphis Compress and Storage, Crump visited the fairgrounds. Shocked at the conditions, Crump sent a telegram to Overton bitterly complaining about the treatment of the refugees.

He wrote:

> *It is criminal on our part to pack all of those people—men, women and children—like sardines in a box at the Fairgrounds. <u>Seeing once is better than being told a thousand times</u>. Please give positive instructions today for the removal of 1500 to 2000 to some school building. They sleep in the same clothes—the women and children in the casino are forced to walk at least a one-quarter of a mile for meals. No extra clothing and if it is raining and cold there they are with wet clothes to sleep in. <u>Horrible condition</u>. Further, there are up in the hundreds on the sick list that should be sent to some hospital. Please let's not postpone this another hour. It is too important—not only for the poor sick, but for the citizens of Memphis. While everybody is doing what they can, let's by all means do this.*[170]

Crump had no knowledge of the plans to begin moving the refugees out of town and use the schools as hospitals. The condition of the Red Cross camp reinforced his doubts about the mayor's handling of the crisis.

Overton responded three days later:

> *I do not think it was criminal to put the people in the Fairgrounds because there was no other place to put them. It would have been criminal to keep them there. We didn't. We all deeply appreciate that if we had known what was coming we would have been prepared. No one has helped more than you have, and we now think we are organized to meet the future with hospitals, doctors, nurses, barracks, food, transportation, medical supplies and whatever is needed.*[171]

Crump had already moved on to what he saw as the main problem areas by the time he received Overton's letter. Crump briefly supervised activities at the North Memphis Pumping Station before personally taking charge of all activities along the Nonconnah Creek where floodwater already covered much of the Standard Oil Company property. Crump, dressed in high-laced boots, red and black plaid pants and a brilliant green jacket, spent hours every day in February at the Nonconnah levee. Crump had concerns about the possible loss of prestige to Memphis if the flood significantly damaged the city and its newly acquired businesses. He did not want Memphians to worry about the levees, and he certainly did not want stories of Memphis flooding appearing on the national press. When asked about levee operations and possible flooding, he curtly told reporters, "Of course Memphis itself is high and dry but there is no need in having such a story hurt the town for years when it can be stopped." Crump said later, "Aside from the damage it [flooding along the Nonconnah] would have caused, it would have meant there had been a levee break in Memphis and we'd had bad publicity all over the country."[172]

Crump caused more problems with the mayor when he ordered city engineer William Fowler to leave the Gayoso Pumping Station and help him take command of the levee crews. As high winds caused waves to splash over the top, it soon became clear that the crews could not build the levee up fast enough to keep pace with the increasing water pressure. Fowler successfully arranged for more manpower, sandbags, trucks and boats. He increased the crews to about two thousand men, mostly from the WPA, and added a night crew of about eight hundred. He managed to help save the day but having to answer to Crump left him in a difficult position with the mayor; Fowler did not receive authorization from Overton to leave his assigned post. Overton, unaware that Fowler had gone to Nonconnah Creek, thought Fowler simply did not show up for work. The furious Overton could not find Fowler so he fired him. The engineer finally made contact with Overton and tried to explain what happened. The mayor withdrew the termination once he calmed down and realized what happened. Even so, the incident caused yet another rift between the mayor and the boss.[173]

The Nonconnah Levee, an embankment less than two miles long between the north side of the creek and the property of the South Memphis Land Company, provided the area with only a minimal amount of protection. The nearby warehouses and plants had some additional flood protection, including small levees, waterproofed walls and blocked windows and doors, but not enough to withstand the coming flood. As early as January 15, pressure from backwater threatened to rupture the levee. Assistant city engineer Thomas E. Maxson said, "That levee was breathing; you could see it moving from the pressure of the water. We were afraid it was going to blow." By January 29, weaknesses appeared in three sections as water came within two feet of the top of the levee. Workers used hundreds of trucks sent by the state highway department and boats from the Red Cross and others recently built at Whitehaven School to carry dirt-filled bags to crews working to reinforce the levee.[174]

Crews consisted of over a thousand WPA workers and more than two hundred prisoners from the penal farm directed by Superintendent Squire

High Water Blues

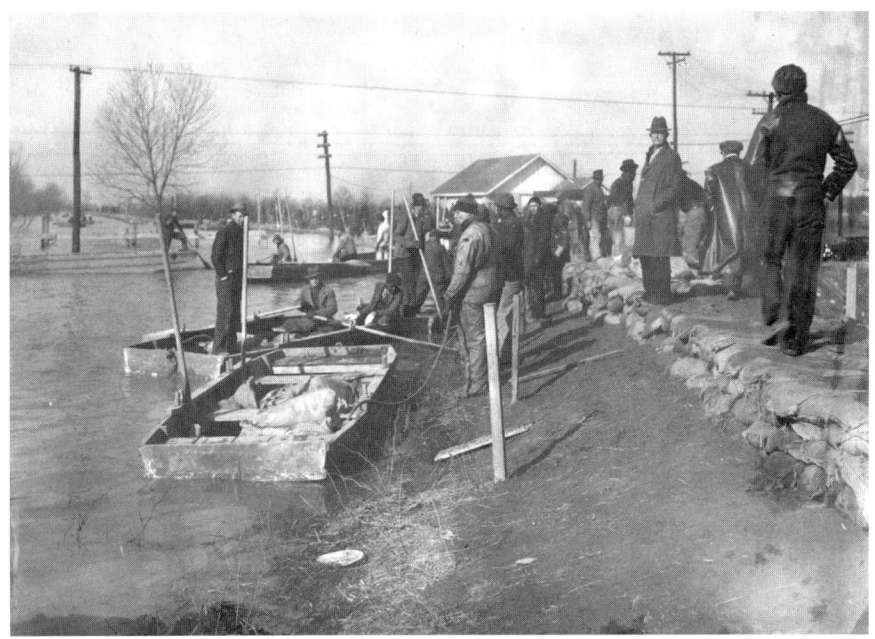

Workers transport sandbags to the Nonconnah levee. *Courtesy of the Memphis and Shelby County Room, Memphis Public Library and Information Center.*

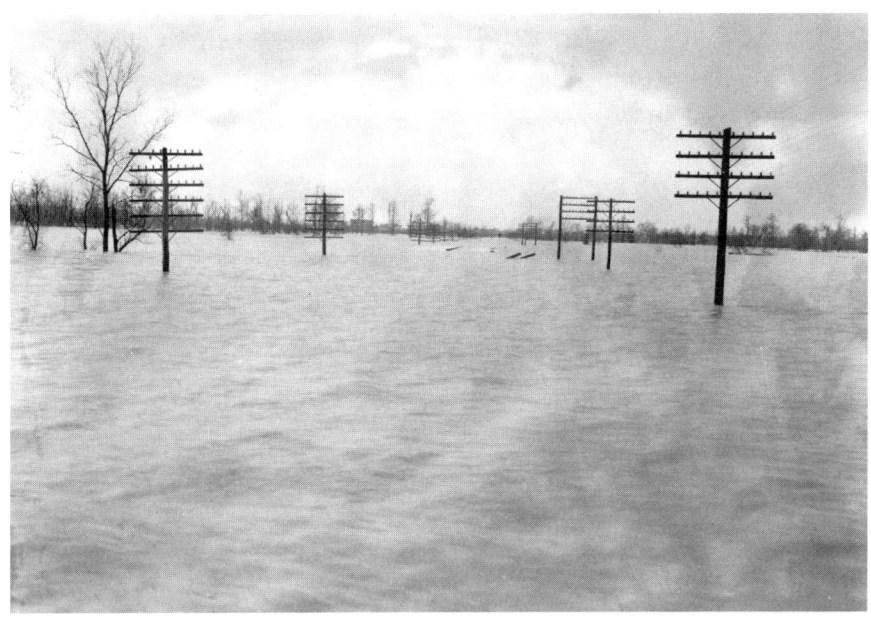

Backwater from the Nonconnah Creek covers Horn Lake Road. *Courtesy of the Memphis and Shelby County Room, Memphis Public Library and Information Center.*

Kearney worked in the rain and mud until nightfall. The levee crews worked hard but steadily fell behind due to a lack of organization and trained boatmen. The WPA added a thousand more workers on January 30 as winds caused water to splash over the fifty-one-foot levee. Even so, the rising water of the Nonconnah still threatened to overwhelm them.[175]

Crump, desperate for more manpower, recruited about five hundred more inmates from the Shelby County Penal Farm to work on the levees in South Memphis. The *Commercial Appeal* reported that the convicts "worked like children at play" after Crump told them he would personally ask Governor Browning to reduce their sentences. Although the convicts probably did not feel overjoyed to work long hours in the cold and rain, Crump followed through with his promise. Once they returned to the penal farm following the passing of the flood crest, guards at roll call read from a list of those who worked hardest at the levee. As the men responded, guards removed the chains from their legs, setting them free.[176]

The releases made the prisoners happy but the news coverage probably left Crump somewhat chagrined. Crump's efforts to encourage the men to work harder may have saved Memphians from being "embarrassed" by the high water, but the stories in national publications of prisoners in leg irons forced to work on the levee did little to help the city's provincial image. A critical *Press Scimitar* reporter wrote, "Others will regret it for the bad advertising that resulted when pictures of convicts in irons toting heavy bags of sand were printed in newspapers and magazines with nation-wide circulation. Such pictures give a bad impression of the community because they portray a practice that cannot be defended."[177]

The indefensible practice of using prisoners in leg irons paled in comparison to the forced conscription of civilians into labor gangs. At some point in early February police received orders go to Beale Street (known as Beale Avenue at the time) to round up African American men for levee work. Thomas Doyle, a writer for the *Crisis*, explained how the reputation of the famous center of African American business and culture attracted the ire of local law enforcement. He described the street as a "hive of respectability by day" with bankers, insurance officers, barbers, dentists and "a zealous group of ministers catering to the material and spiritual needs of the community." However, pastors complained that by night Beale Street harbored too many camouflaged bordellos and that gambling and drinking too often caused knifings and murders. The street's nighttime reputation kept black leaders "in a state of constant anxiety" and gave police the justification they felt they needed for brutality that extended beyond Beale. Doyle wrote, "Policing is

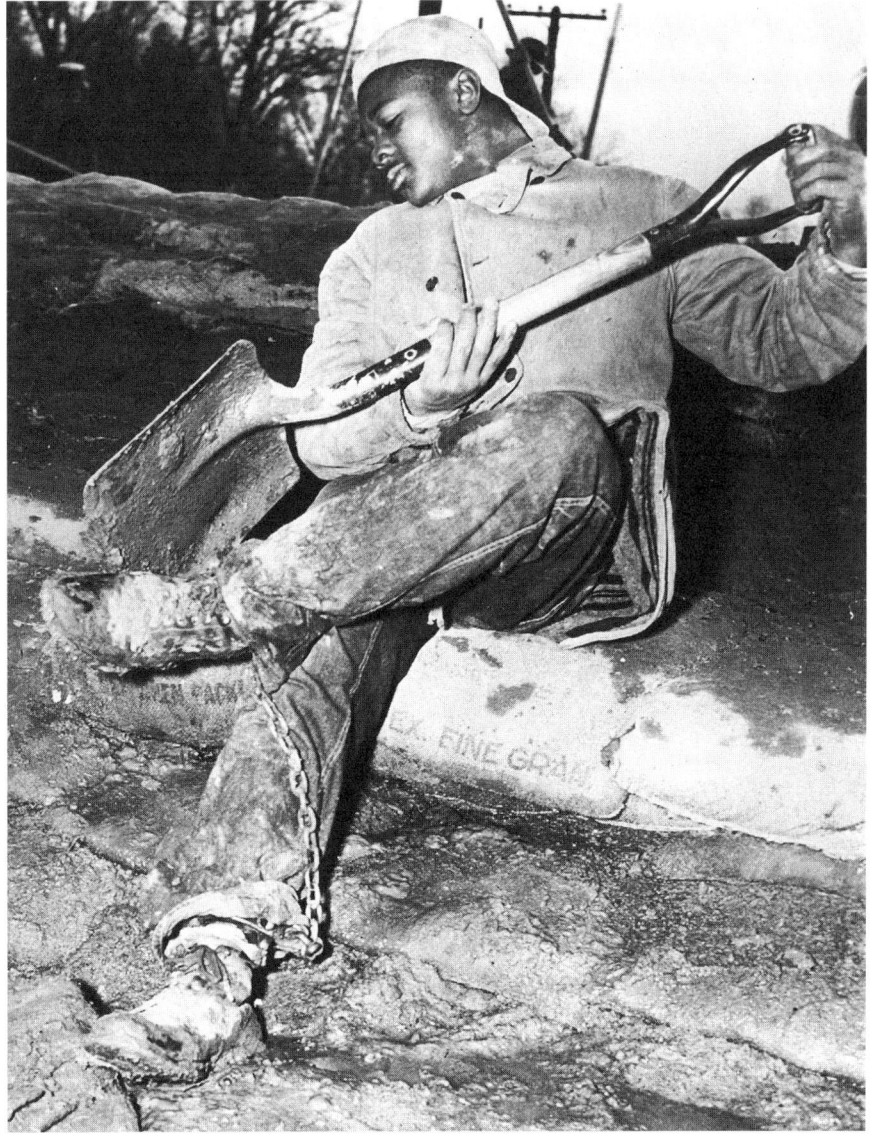

Shelby County Penal Farm inmate cleans mud from his boots while working on Nonconnah levee. *Courtesy of the Associated Press.*

mostly in the hands of Mississipians, who are known to be uncompromisingly stern in their handling of Negro miscreants. In this area more than any other, charges have been made of discrimination and undue severity in the treatment of Negro suspects."[178]

MEMPHIS AND THE SUPERFLOOD OF 1937

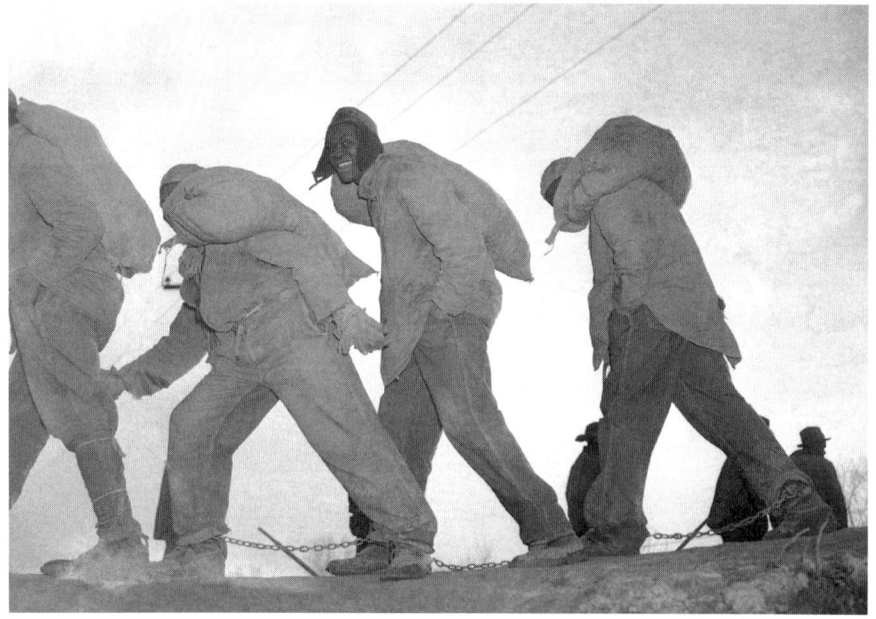

Chain gang carrying sandbags to Nonconnah levee. *Courtesy of the Associated Press.*

Officers in police cars, followed by trucks, went to Beale Street and rounded up African American men from the street, theaters, pool halls and restaurants and forced them into work details. Police emptied the well-known lunch counter, One Minute Lunch, and waited outside the doors to movie theaters and took men as they exited, separating them from wives and girlfriends. Some couples refused to exit and stayed in theaters all night until the police left.[179]

Police loaded up men eighteen to a truck and took them directly to camps near the Nonconnah. It made no difference what they wore—whether in overalls or expensive suits, spats or bowlers—they all had to go. Police forced the men to work in the mud without gloves and in their good clothes, ruining suits, shoes, shirts and overcoats.[180]

Conscripts worked twelve-hour shifts loading one-hundred-pound sandbags while penal farm inmates and white workers had the easier job of simply filling the bags. They reported being "cursed out, brow-beaten, and eged [sic] to greater effort at the point of guns." Volunteer workers received thirty-five cents an hour while conscripts only received twenty-seven cents an hour. Overseers allowed white workers to warm themselves occasionally by fires as they kept the men from Beale in the cold and beat a number of them with sticks. Lieutenant George W. Lee, chairman of the voluntary recruitment of African Americans for flood work, met with the police to discuss the overall treatment of African Americans and the forced labor problem. Eventually, after the flood crest passed, the police agreed to ease up on the treatment of the workers and end the practice of forced conscription.[181]

Roy Wilkins, editor of the *Crisis* and future executive secretary of the NAACP, interviewed police commissioner Davis about the treatment of the conscripted workers. Davis claimed that he stopped the shanghaiing of men from Beale once he became aware of the situation but would not say who gave the orders that started the practice. He suggested off-handedly that "some deputy sheriff from out in the country got excited, came into town and got some policemen to help him round up men." Wilkins asked if county deputies had this kind of authority over city police officers but Davis, absorbed with lighting a new cigar, ignored the question.[182]

Wilkins obviously assumed the order originated with the police commissioner. However, the order most likely came from someone supervising work crews at the Nonconnah levee and only Crump had enough clout to order police to do such a thing. Understandably, Davis refused to answer questions about who gave the order; he would never say anything to embarrass the boss by implicating him in the matter.

Memphians anxiously followed the reports from Reybold's office of the approaching flood crest. They predicted its arrival on February 8, but the water continued to rise through the next day, which was accompanied by high winds and a burst of rain. Workers saw whitecaps three or four feet high in the Memphis harbor at the height of the storm as gusts of wind momentarily reached forty miles an hour. By 2:45 p.m., the waves began to subside as the wind veered from the south to northwest. The storm passed but the river continued to rise, upsetting predictions of river forecasters. It continued up the gauges by fractions of an inch until it finally crested on February 10.[183]

Crump never wanted Memphians to have to struggle to save the city from flooding again; he considered it embarrassing and bad for business. He thought about improving flood protection for the city as he diligently directed levee work on Nonconnah Creek.

He sent a telegram to his good friend and political ally Senator Kenneth McKellar:

> *"I must stick it out here on the Nonconnah levee we hope to hold it. Please keep this in mind, levees, pumping stations, and seawalls should*

MEMPHIS AND THE SUPERFLOOD OF 1937

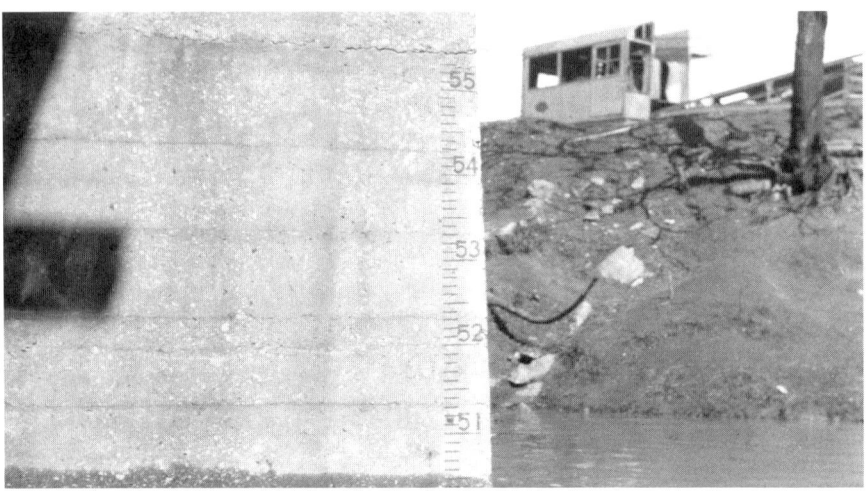

River gauge at Memphis at flood crest. *Courtesy of the Memphis and Shelby County Room, Memphis Public Library and Information Center.*

be built around Memphis to prevent a recurrence of floodwaters from the Mississippi, Nonconnah, and Wolf Rivers. Levees are built all over the United States on rivers to protect towns and farms, why not Louisville, Memphis, and other cities?" [184]

Reybold announced that the flood had officially ended for Memphis on February 18. However, plenty of work remained. Engineers closed the Bird's Point–New Madrid Floodway to block the river so the farmers could return and begin their spring planting. Four thousand men used earth-moving machines, trucks, tractors, scrapers and sandbags to construct the largest ring levee ever in the United States. Engineers auctioned off rubber boats, raincoats and similar items while they gave leftover johnboats to various levee districts. Also, workers continued to clean up debris before refugees could be returned to their homes.[185]

The Memphis Red Cross spent about $255,000 on the care of refugees by February 20 and it was not over. Even as one hundred families a day left refugee centers, Memphians now had to care for the refugees returning from the camps east of the city. Officials set up facilities, cots and hot meals at the fairgrounds once again to accommodate the Arkansans traveling through Memphis back home.[186]

Many worried about the next flood and what it would do to the city. Even with the opening of the Bird's Point–New Madrid Floodway the Mississippi

High Water Blues

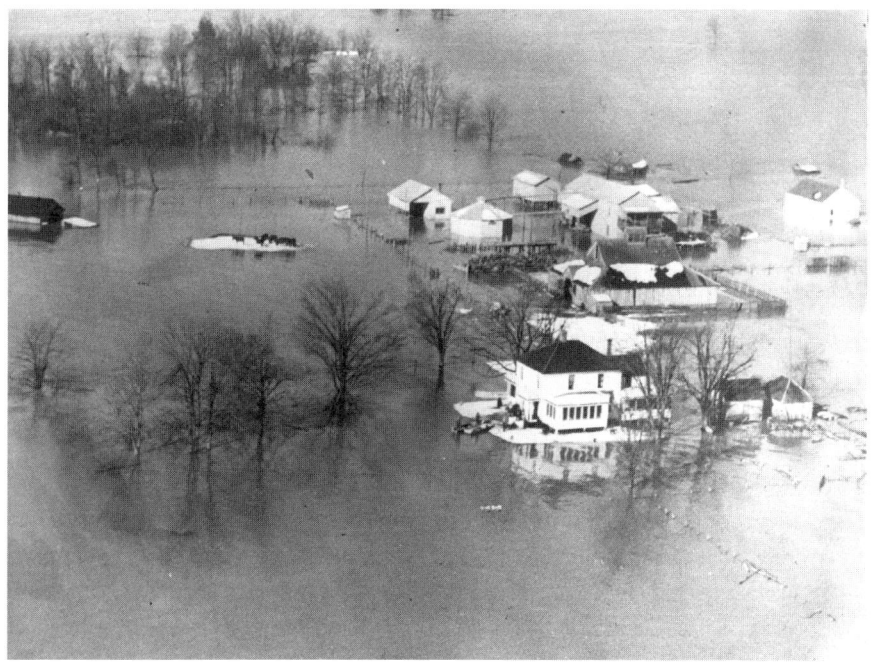

Flooded homes in the Bird's Point–New Madrid Floodway. *Courtesy of the University of Memphis Special Collections.*

River at Memphis crested at an all-time record of 48.7 feet (50.4 feet on the old gauge), causing about $300,000 in property damage. In addition, Memphians had to care for over 60,000 refugees, 150 of whom died here. The flood had such an impact on Memphis that Mayor Overton's flood committee became a permanent institution with twenty-eight subcommittees. People did not consider the events of 1927 and 1937 as aberrations but rather the beginning of a trend of superfloods. City leaders wanted to prepare for the next disaster, but preparations required large-scale operations. The only way they could achieve their goal was with federal funding but getting that money proved more difficult than expected.[187]

The president's attention on the vast devastation of the flood gave Crump the chance to fulfill his longtime goal of comprehensive flood control for the city. Crump knew that the best way to get federal flood-control funding was to have a good flood, so he put his men to work in Washington before the crest even passed. Chandler and McKellar submitted bills to the U.S. Congress while Crump's secretary, Marvin Pope, worked behind the scenes urging southern congressmen, including House flood-control chairman

William Whittington of Mississippi to support the inclusion of funding for the city.

Even so, Crump's men encountered considerable resistance. Roosevelt wanted to focus efforts on the Ohio Valley, warning Whittington that he would veto any bill with a single item affecting the Mississippi River. Others resented the requests for further flood control funding for the Mississippi Valley.

Indiana's Representative Glenn Griswold complained:

> *Why was not something like that done about the Ohio? It was stupid to build levees on the Mississippi to hold floods which rose and did their first damage on the Ohio…It seems to me that Congressmen from the South have been less interested in Mississippi flood control as a problem than in having flood control funds spent in their own section.*[188]

Crump would not take no for an answer and had Senator McKellar, Representative Walter Chandler and other supporters continue lobbying. Meanwhile, Crump's health took a turn for the worse because of the time he spent in the rain at the Nonconnah levee, so he booked a room at the Arlington Hotel in Hot Springs, Arkansas, on February 15 to get away from Memphis and recover. He returned at the end of March but left again for his favorite sanatorium in Battle Creek, Michigan, leaving the difficult legislative battle to the senior members of his machine.

IT'S IN THE BAG

The best means of getting federal flood control money is to have a good flood.
—Time *magazine, February 1, 1937*[189]

Local and federal agencies, professionals and volunteers all worked together with a remarkable sense of camaraderie and cooperation during the flood crisis. However, building a consensus to create a new comprehensive flood-control project for Memphis proved far more challenging. Crump insisted on taking charge during the height of the flood crisis but left local politicians to take on the responsibility of securing funding afterward. However, as much as one might have complained about Crump's heavy-handed tactics in dealing with his subordinates, it became obvious in his absence that his machine could not run without his direct input.

Crump had wanted federally funded flood control for Memphis since his involvement in the floods of 1912 and 1913, and he knew that the current flood might give him that opportunity if he could find just the right opening. Lieutenant Colonel Reybold gave reason to hope when he telephoned Fowler, asking for any plan he had in mind for flood protection for Memphis and to include any recommendations in his report to General Markham. Fowler's office completed preliminary plans and estimates for new flood-control measures for the city on February 15. Fowler met with Reybold for four hours on February 17 and discussed the plan in detail. Reybold assured him that he would pass along his recommendations to Markham. In a telephone call several days later, Reybold again promised that new flood-control measures would have ample provision for Memphis.[190]

A young assistant engineer and draftsman named Thomas E. Maxson, who worked under Fowler, developed the new plan. Maxson, who eventually became the city engineer in 1962, wrote a report analyzing the effects of the flood on the city and suggesting what to do to prepare for the next superflood. Maxson insisted Memphis needed the flood protection program. He wrote, "Undoubtedly, from a viewpoint of economic stability, safety and public health, and common humanity, a program of adequate flood protection for the City of Memphis should be undertaken and pushed to a completion." Floodwater from the Ohio Valley caused the flood crest at Memphis to come within 1.6 feet of the tops of the highest levees. Maxson worried that another superflood with drainage from both the Ohio and upper Mississippi Valleys would surely overtake current flood protection for the city.[191]

Maxson identified three trouble areas: North Memphis–Wolf River Basin, the Gayoso Basin and South Memphis–Nonconnah Creek Basin. His plan included adding more pumping stations and the construction of "seawalls with an average height of thirty feet set on a continuous row of steel sheet piling with an average penetration of thirty-five feet." He pointed out the flood could have been much worse since it resulted from overflow from the Ohio River with little coming from the upper Mississippi and Missouri Rivers. He believed Memphis should be prepared for the possibility of all three flooding, causing a disaster to rival the 1937 flood.

He wrote:

> *The fact that the 1937 flood reached a stage of 50.4 feet at Memphis or 3.8 feet above any previous record and reached 1.6 feet of the top of the North Memphis Levee must necessarily call for a revision of our estimate as to the stage of a possible super flood in Memphis. As a minimum stage to be used in estimating the effects of a super flood on the city of Memphis the stage set by the U. S. Engineers as having been possible during the recent flood that of 55 will be used in assembling the data contained herein.* [192]

The North Memphis System consisted of both the North Memphis–Wolf River and Gayoso Bayou Basins. The North Memphis–Wolf River Basin covered 3,051 acres with about 40 industrial and manufacturing plants and over 4,000 homes and storage buildings valued at over $18 million. City planners expected this highly valued area to continue to develop as an industrial center. The Gayoso Bayou Basin covered a 452-acre area with 1,365 homes, 33 manufacturing plants as well as over 200 businesses, schools, fire stations, federally funded public housing, St. Joseph's Hospital and 50 churches valued at over $24 million.[193]

Maxson's plan for the North Memphis System called for the sea wall to begin at the foot of Jefferson Street and extend north along the Memphis Harbor to North Second Street. The wall would then continue along the bluffs east almost to National Cemetery. Even if a sea wall could not span the entire distance, he hoped to at least have it extend to the lake on the Missouri Portland Sand and Gravel Company property and the rest of the distance could be covered by an earth levee. He recommended that engineers place new pumping stations, floodgates and reservoirs along the Marble Street Drainage Ditch, Sunflower Bayou, Cypress Creek, Lick Creek, Leath Bayou, Workhouse Creek and National Cemetery Creek. Maxson also pointed out the need to upgrade the Gayoso Pumping Station and to improve North Memphis drainage structures, including rerouting some bayous and changing surface drain inlets in order to prevent backwater from going into interceptors and surface drains.[194]

The South Memphis System desperately needed a permanent levee. The 1,789-acre area contained twenty industrial plants and about three hundred homes and small storage buildings valued at over $5 million. In addition, the area provided land for future industrial and railroad expansion. The makeshift levee in that area would not withstand another sustained flood stage and little had been done to prevent backwater along its tributaries. To solve these problems, Maxson wanted to place a pumping station at the mouth of the Mallory Bayou and an intercepting channel in the Cane Creek Basin. He also wanted a combination of concrete sea walls and an improved earth levee along the Nonconnah Creek like those in the North Memphis System.[195]

Maxson argued that a superflood with a flood stage of fifty-five feet or more would cause economic distress, sewage problems and inhibit the city's ability to act as a safe haven for refugees. He estimated that such a flood would cause property damage to businesses and residential areas that would leave thirty thousand homeless and unemployed. The Gayoso pumping station, which handled the majority of the city's sewage, would shut down. Sewage would back up into homes and businesses and cause a health crisis. These problems would have far-reaching effects.

Maxson wrote:

> *Thus the problem of flood control in Memphis becomes one of concern for the entire lower valley as this haven of refuge is being threatened by the continued raising of the maximum flood stages through the construction of larger and higher confining levees throughout the entire length of the Mississippi River and its tributaries.*[196]

Overton and Fowler presented the plan to Reybold with the expectation that Markham would automatically approve it. In the meantime, Overton discussed flood protection for Memphis with Harry Hopkins and General Markham in person during their visit to Memphis. The two however gave Overton only a lukewarm response, saying that the federal government only had money available for upgrading the mainline levees. Overton began to have misgivings about Reybold's assurances and appealed to Senator McKellar to speak to Markham on the matter.[197]

Fowler, who never received a copy of Reybold's report, wrote to General Fergusson to verify the proposed flood control included provisions for Memphis. Major R.G. Moses responded on behalf of Fergusson, saying any plan for Memphis should fall under future plans for the overall region. He wrote, "It would therefore appear that discussion of a definite and detailed plan such as you propose for Memphis would be premature at this time." Overton responded by requesting a personal meeting with Fergusson. Fergusson hoped to avoid the Memphians and had his office respond by saying he had left Vicksburg and would not return until the following week.[198]

In Washington, Congressman Walter Chandler began pressing the issue of including provisions for Memphis in the upcoming flood-control bill. He worked for weeks on securing funding for PWA projects in Memphis for schools and drainage before the bill came about. He lobbied for funds to improve sewage in North Memphis and approached the president on February 20 about the creation of a PWA project to build an intercepting sewer to relieve pollution in the Wolf River. As the flood crisis developed, he began turning his focus on the inclusion of provisions for Memphis in the new flood-control bill at Crump's insistence.[199]

On April 20, Chandler notified Overton that General Harley B. Fergusson, president of the Mississippi River Commission, now supported and recommended the adoption of the Memphis Flood Control Plan. The formalized plan called for the federal expenditure of $8,733,000, including $1,000,000 for revetment of the Wolf River with a contribution of

High Water Blues

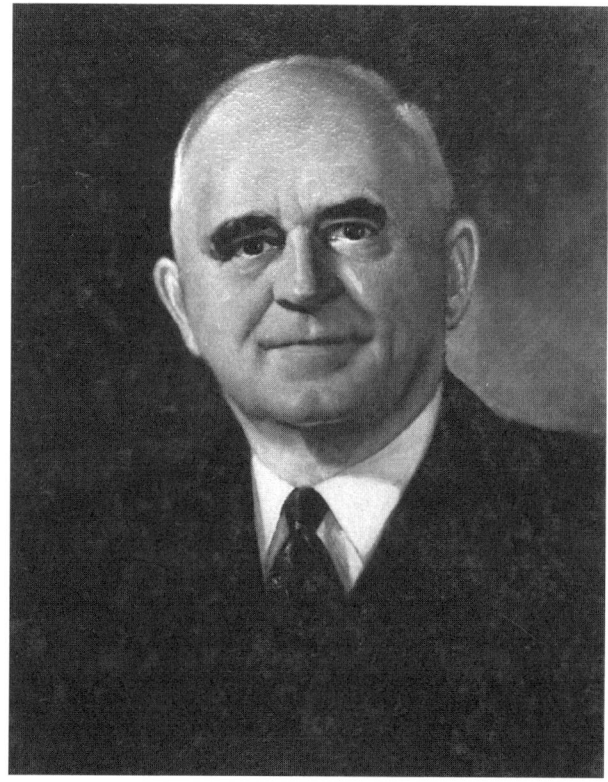

Walter Chandler served in the United States Congress for five years before becoming mayor of Memphis in 1940 and 1955. *Courtesy of the Memphis and Shelby County Room, Memphis Public Library and Information Center.*

approximately $3,000,000. Chandler then had to convince the House Flood Control Committee to adopt the plan. Overton offered his congratulations and wrote that he had given "the biggest news that Memphis could receive!"[200]

The House Committee on Flood Control began hearings for flood protection in the Ohio Valley on June 7. Chairman William Whittington advised Chandler that Congress would not take up the matter of relief for towns and cities on the Mississippi River until it reconvened in January since Roosevelt requested that the committee limit itself to the Ohio Valley. Chandler remained optimistic however since he now had the cooperation of Markham.[201]

On June 15, Chandler made a passionate plea to Congress to support the inclusion of provisions for Memphis in the new flood-control bill, emphasizing that the Mississippi River Commission, corps of engineers and War Department had approved the plan. The revised plan would cost approximately $12,000,000 with a contribution of $3,400,000 from Memphis and Shelby County. He summarized the efforts of Memphians in the recent disaster and emphasized the need to ensure it remains a safe haven for refugees. He compared the exodus of eastern Arkansas to the Belgians who fled their homes as invading German troops approached in 1914. Everyone expected sanctuary in Memphis as others before them had for over a hundred years. However, the superfloods threatened the city's ability to care for refugees. The next one could easily overwhelm current levees and pumping stations that would not only damage the city but also inhibit its ability to act as the regional relief headquarters.

Chandler stated:

> *For value received alone during the recent flood alone, the federal government should compensate the city of Memphis by providing permanent protection for its outlying sections, thereby leaving its citizens free to concentrate their attention and resources on the far greater task of caring for the refugees who come from every nook and corner of the lowlands.*[202]

Whittington met with Chandler again and reaffirmed the president's desire to focus only on the Ohio Valley. Chandler told him that he had several witnesses from Memphis he wanted to testify before the committee and that Fowler's plans had the approval of every agency but Congress. Chandler had pushed the issue to the point of "becoming a nuisance." Whittington met with Roosevelt and tried to push the issue of providing better flood protection for Memphis, as well as Cairo and other Mississippi Valley cities, but the president resisted. The chairman assured Chandler he would do all he could for Memphis, and the congressman had nothing left to do but wait.[203]

The final push for the legislation depended on McKellar, the veteran Memphis senator who wielded significant influence in the capital. During his early days in Congress, McKellar in 1916 persuaded President Woodrow Wilson to support federal highway legislation that distributed $75 million to the states. McKellar found political success by using federal money to promote economic development in the states, especially in Tennessee where he controlled the jobs that came with the funding. In his first years in the Senate, McKellar supported President Wilson's progressive reform program and his unsuccessful attempt to convince the Senate to ratify the Treaty of Versailles. McKellar supported progressive legislation and insisted that, despite the nation's general prosperity, Tennessee and the South needed federal economic aid through the 1920s. McKellar won re-election in 1922 and then defeated House Democratic leader Finis Garrett in 1928.[204]

High Water Blues

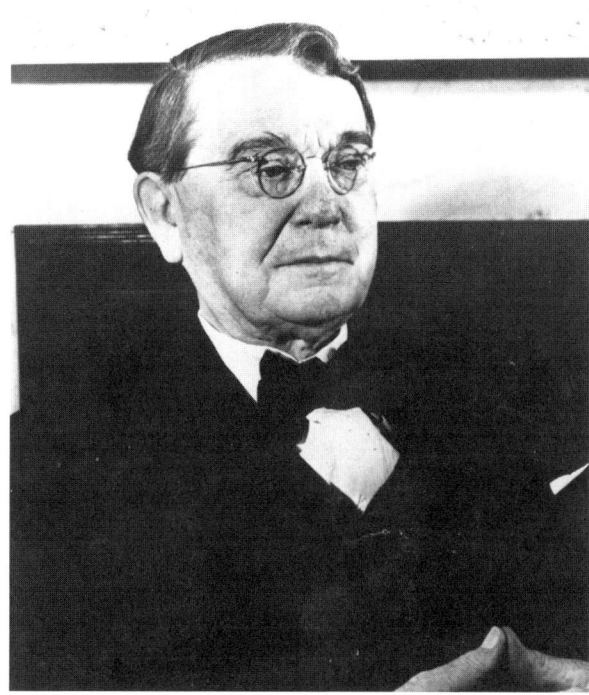

Senator Kenneth Douglas McKellar. *Courtesy of the Memphis and Shelby County Room, Memphis Public Library and Information Center.*

McKellar's growing seniority following his re-elections paid off with the election of Franklin Roosevelt in 1932 and the launch of the New Deal. McKellar controlled countless jobs through federal programs that operated under the New Deal because of his seniority as chairman of the Senate Committee on Post Office and Post Roads and as a ranking member of the Senate Appropriations Committee. McKellar supported federal aid for farmers and New Deal relief programs and helped lead the fight in Congress for the Tennessee Valley Authority Act in 1933. [205]

Roosevelt, though reluctant to authorize funding for flood control in the South, respected McKellar and recognized his expertise on matters of flood control for years. In 1927, Roosevelt wrote to the senator, asking for his views on the Mississippi Valley Flood. He thought that President Coolidge and his advisors had downplayed the severity of the flood for political reasons and wanted McKellar to clarify the situation. He also asked about the practicability of leaders of both parties in the Senate and House to make an agreement to make flood relief and prevention the focus of a special session of Congress. [206]

On August 10, Roosevelt began to consider supporting the inclusion of provisions for Memphis in the coming legislation. However, Whittington remained doubtful and wrote to Overton that the bill probably would not include works for Memphis. A few days later, McKellar succeeded in getting the amendment authorizing the work at Memphis on the bill. Whittington worried that Congress would balk since it would appear that Memphis would receive appropriations to the exclusion of other important points along the Mississippi River. Chandler asked Overton for assistance in asking key figures, such as Ed Crump, to telegram Whittington and express their views on the regional importance of Memphis.[207]

The flood-control plan for Memphis hung in the balance as the congressional session approached its closing days. McKellar stepped in and used his influence to help out, playing an instrumental role in the closing hours by having the $9 million appropriation inserted in the general deficiency bill. The bill passed on August 21 and the president signed it into law on August 28. Reporter Thomas Fauntleroy announced "it's in the bag!" Congress did not provide appropriations until the following January but jubilant engineers immediately began planning the largest construction project in the city's history.[208]

The congressional session closed and Chandler, after three months, finally got to return to Memphis to see his wife and children. One would have expected a warm welcome after all his efforts, but city politicians greeted him with anger and disappointment. Overton and Fowler certainly appreciated Chandler's efforts with the flood-control legislation but they did not want to see him come home. They expected the congressman to remain in Washington to try to secure funding for PWA work in Memphis even though Congress had adjourned. Weeks earlier, the impatient Overton traveled to Washington with the city attorney and engineer to try to secure PWA funding without Chandler's input or help. Having little understanding of the legislative process, they left empty-handed after only five days.[209]

Overton and Fowler became furious when they heard that Chandler planned to return to Memphis. Fowler accused the congressman of not following through with his job of securing PWA funding. Overton said, "I sent Congressman Chandler several wires expressing the importance of our program, only to learn he had departed for Memphis before a single project on our list had received official approval, at the very time projects for other cities were being announced daily and other congressmen were on the job." Sadly, Crump's most important men continued to bicker until the boss returned from his stay in Battle Creek to settle the dispute.[210]

Fortunately, the Memphis, Wolf River and Nonconnah Creek Tennessee Flood Control Project proceeded as scheduled with congressional

High Water Blues

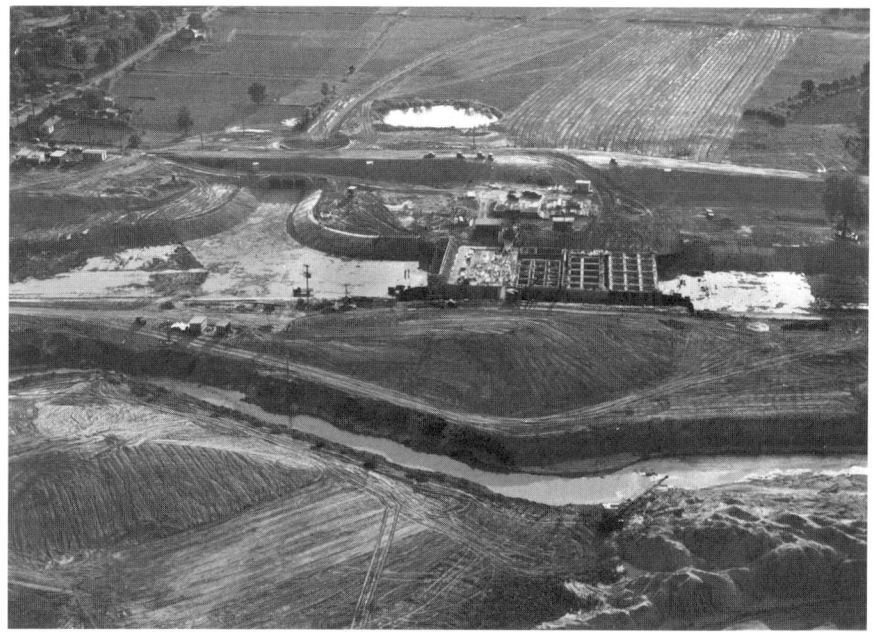

Construction of the Cypress Creek Pumping Station. *Courtesy of the University of Memphis Special Collections.*

amendments on June 28, 1939, and July 24, 1946. It provided for the construction of new levees, floodwalls, drainage structures and bank protection works to withstand a fifty-five-foot flood crest as recommended by Maxson. The principal features included about three miles of floodwall, six miles of earthen levee along the left bank of the Wolf River between Jefferson Avenue and Douglas Park and about four miles of earthen levee on the right banks of the Nonconnah Creek and Cane Creek to a point near Mallory Avenue. The project also included eight storage reservoirs, one pumping station for interior drainage, two for the disposal of sewage and three as a combination of both. Federal funds paid for the construction of retaining walls and earthen levees along the Wolf River and Nonconnah Creek, while municipal funds paid for the additional pumping stations.[211]

The Ohio–Mississippi Valley Flood of 1937 not only proved the measures brought about by the 1928 Flood Control Act worked, but it also emphasized the need for more governmental conservation and flood-control projects. The mainline levees and spillways functioned well, but the lack of adequate levees and pumping stations along the tributaries allowed backwater to cause a great deal of damage. The event underscored the need for continued federal reforestation and flood-control projects on tributaries in the Ohio and Mississippi Valleys. As one *Time* magazine reporter wrote: "The best means of getting Federal flood control money is to have a good flood." Indeed, improved media coverage and communications allowed Americans and the world a front-row seat to the devastation of the flood, forcing the U.S. government to take responsibility and act accordingly. The passage of the flood-control bill paved the way for furthering the flood-protection program still in existence today.[212]

EPILOGUE

*How wisely fate ordain'd for human kind
Calamity! which is the perfect glass,
Wherein we truly see and know ourselves.*
—*William Davenant*[213]

The Red Cross called the Ohio–Mississippi Valley Flood of 1937 "the worst [natural] disaster in the history of the nation." The organization spent an amount nearly equal to what it spent on the Mississippi Valley Flood of 1927 and the Drought of 1930–1931 combined. The flood affected 196 counties in 12 states from West Virginia to Louisiana, with an additional 144 counties involved in sheltering refugees. The Red Cross provided assistance to 59,560 landowners and 193,506 renters, and its camps provided shelter and rescue teams transported the stranded to safety, preventing large-scale loss of life.[214]

Even so, 137 people reportedly died directly as a result of the flood and another 544 received injuries in the Ohio and Mississippi Valleys. However, the Red Cross pointed out that these statistics "while reasonably accurate, are not to be taken as completely correct. In some instances it was difficult to determine whether a death or injury should be charged to the flood or to other causes."[215]

The exact number of flood-related deaths remains unclear in Memphis. During the months of January and February of 1937, influenza, pneumonia, bronchitis and upper-respiratory infections caused or contributed to the

Epilogue

deaths of 330 residents and flood refugees in the city. The local health department also reported an additional thirty-seven cases of tuberculosis, two cases of typhoid fever and one of diphtheria that resulted in deaths. Not every death resulted from the flood, but one can reasonably conclude that exposure contributed significantly to these figures.[216]

Reybold announced that the flood had officially ended for Memphis on February 18, even though the Mississippi River remained above flood stage until March 2. The news signaled to the Red Cross and the municipal government to shut down rescue and relief operations and begin its "back home" movement for the flood victims in the camps. The Red Cross returned all city and county schools but Fairview and Carnes Schools by February 15, and George E. Myer, Red Cross regional director, expected to return all the remaining refugees to their homes within two months. The number of homeless flood victims in Memphis had dropped to 2,075, while another 19,980 received aid but stayed with friends or family in the city.[217]

Officials assured anxious Memphians that they planned to return the refugees to their homes in an orderly manner as soon as possible and asked the public for patience. One official said, "We cannot just pick up a family and drop it some other place. We must find out that the family will be

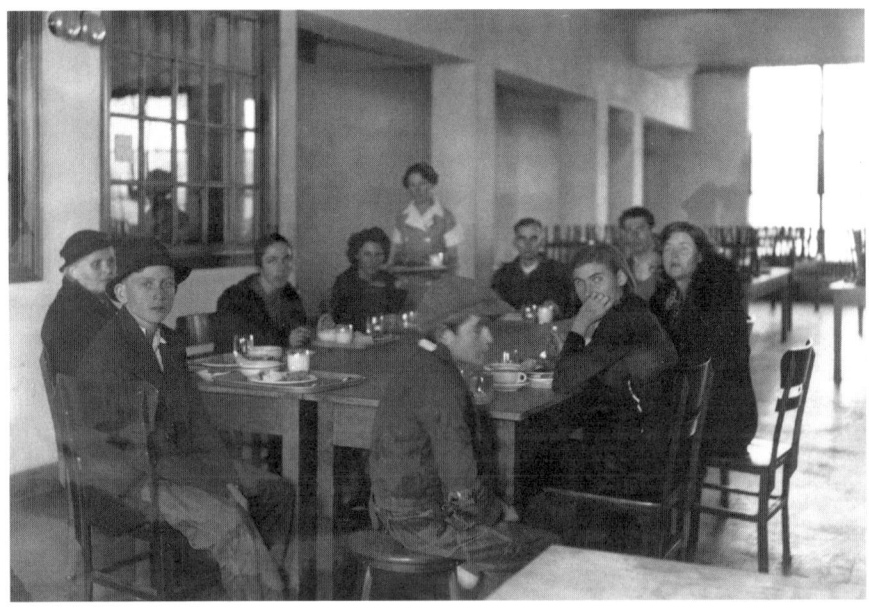

Refugees eating one last meal before they return home. *Courtesy of the Memphis and Shelby County Room, Memphis Public Library and Information Center.*

properly and permanently located back home, and that takes a little time." Doris Thain evaluated the refugees' needs, and Mary Lewis Stone arranged transportation. Stone directed the transportation of over one hundred families per day with the majority of them traveling by automobile or trucks supplied by plantation owners.[218]

The Red Cross not only faced the task of returning the refugees to their homes, but also provided aid to help them rebuild their homes and farms. Myer explained:

> *Every family affected by the disaster and without sufficient resources to re-establish itself unaided will, so far as possible, be given sufficient help so that it may again become self-supporting.* The Red Cross provided aid [rehabilitation] *to refugees based on their need. Myer illustrated the process: "Mr. A and his family have lost everything in the flood—house, furniture, clothing; he has a wife, four small children, and a dependent mother; his bank account is negligible, he has no borrowing power and his income is only sufficient to meet his daily needs. Mr. B and his family likewise have lost everything, but he has a good job, money in the bank and is well able to carry his own burden. Thus it is clear that Mr. A must have help to rebuild and refurnish his house if he is to get back on his feet at all. It is equally clear that Mr. B is in a position to rehabilitate himself without Red Cross aid. The award is made solely upon the basis of need as revealed by the facts our investigation discloses."*[219]

Families receiving aid selected needed items from a merchant who provided them with the cost. The refugees then gave the bill to the Red Cross, who in turn issued disbursement orders to the merchant. The merchant delivered the items, the family signed the receipt and the Red Cross paid the merchant by check once they received the invoice. The Red Cross gave all aid as gifts rather than loans, and they kept all transactions confidential "to avoid embarrassment" to the recipients.[220]

The Mayor's Disaster Committee closed its office in the courthouse on February 15 as Overton and local officials began to focus on the flood-control legislation and returning local flood victims to their homes. The mayor, worried about the condition of homes and businesses in North Memphis, directed the health department to inspect every house in the areas flooded by backwater from the Wolf River and its tributaries. Crews moved out over seven hundred people by February 13 and continued evacuations until the water subsided. The Red Cross assisted over nine hundred families

Epilogue

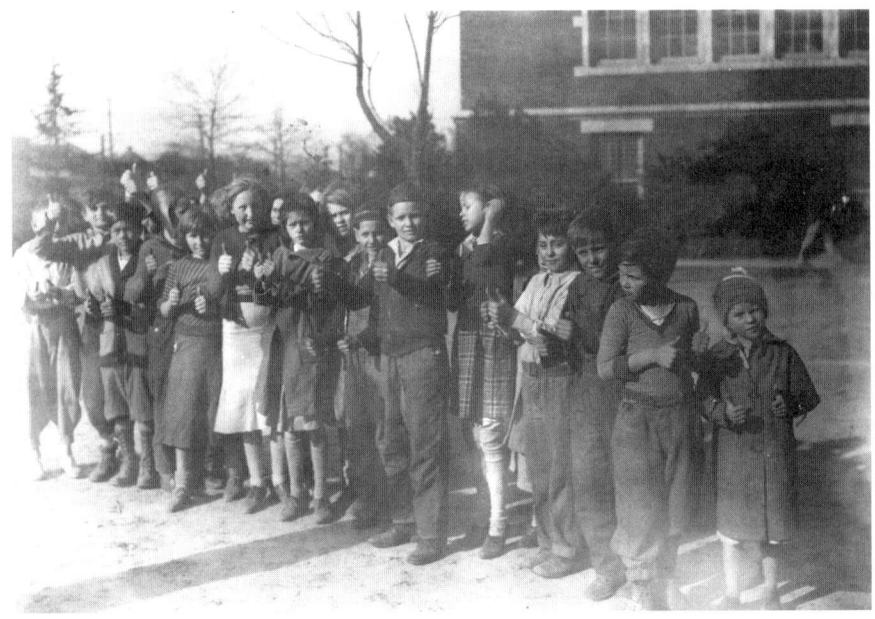

Refugee children give a "thumbs up" at the camp at Fairview School. *Courtesy of the Memphis and Shelby County Room, Memphis Public Library and Information Center.*

from Shelby County during the flood. Health superintendent Dr. L.M. Graves and A.H. Fletcher, sanitary engineer, announced on February 15 that residents in private homes could no longer obtain water from private sources. They required all residents to have a connection to the city water system and sewers before returning to their homes and condemned all private wells and privies.[221]

The armada of personnel and equipment soon disbanded once the crisis ended. The WPA reassigned its personnel, and men and equipment stationed in Memphis by the coast guard and TVA began to return home on February 18. About six hundred TVA employees, 160 vehicles and 75 boats left by the end of the week. Railroad cars carried over one hundred coast guard personnel and 30 boats back to communities as far away as New York, Massachusetts, Rhode Island, Maine and Florida.[222]

Even though the crisis had passed, the corps of engineers of the Memphis district still had plenty of work to do. Over the next month, four thousand men used earth-moving machines, trucks, tractors, scrapers and sandbags to construct the largest ring levee ever in the United States, closing the Bird's Point–New Madrid Floodway. Once completed, farmers soon returned to

Epilogue

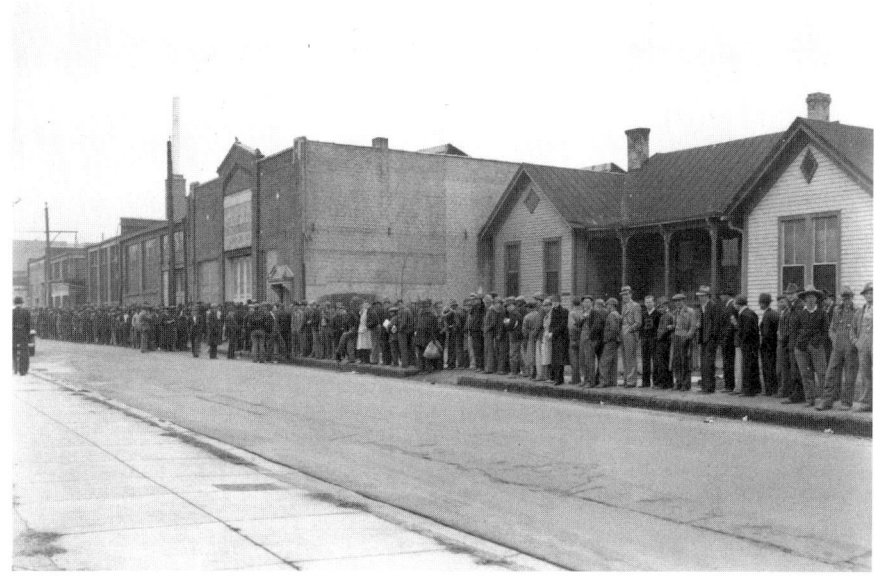

WPA workers line up to receive checks for work done during the flood. *Courtesy of the Memphis and Shelby County Room, Memphis Public Library and Information Center.*

the spillway to clean up debris and begin spring plantings. The engineers then auctioned off rubber boats, raincoats and similar items and gave the leftover johnboats to various levee districts.[223]

The health crisis improved as well. Local doctors cared for nearly two hundred sick babies at the beginning of February but, by the middle of the month, only thirty-two remained under doctors' care. Medical staff returned the children to parents still quarantined at the fairgrounds.[224]

Even as refugees in the city returned home, hundreds refugees from more remote areas in eastern Arkansas continued to come to Memphis through the end of February. The fairgrounds camp eventually closed on March 10, and the city's duties as the regional Red Cross headquarters ended on March 15. The Red Cross kept an office open in the Sterick Building for three more weeks to oversee assistance on the eastern side of the Mississippi Valley while David Jaques supervised rehabilitation to Shelby County residents. A rehabilitation committee met nightly to advise caseworkers on family needs. Hospital staff still cared for 244 refugees, and the 150 remaining family members transferred from the fairgrounds to the Madison Heights School.[225]

The Red Cross offices at the Auditorium closed, and Red Cross director W.I. Jones left for a new assignment helping the Ohio Valley.

Epilogue

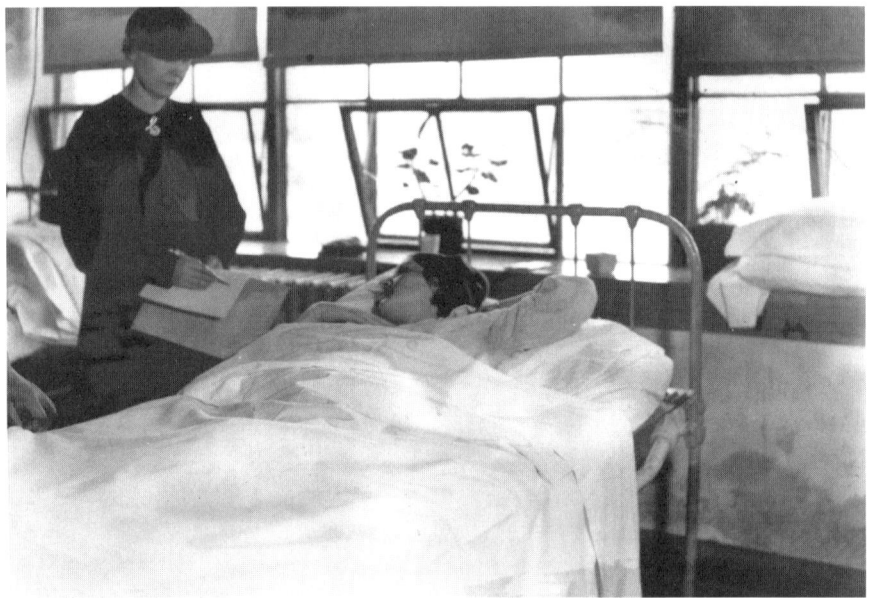

Pneumonia victim recovering after she pulled a boat with her bedridden husband and child three miles through neck-deep water to safety. *Courtesy of the Memphis and Shelby County Room, Memphis Public Library and Information Center.*

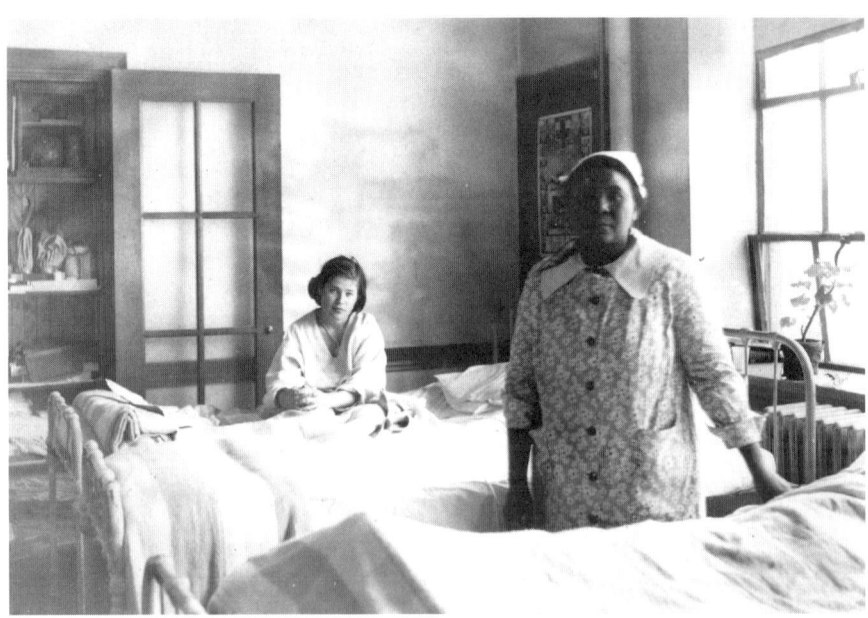

A recovering refugee and a WPA maid at Fairview School. *Courtesy of the Memphis and Shelby County Room, Memphis Public Library and Information Center.*

Epilogue

Jones said:

> *In leaving, I carry with me the highest esteem for the citizens of this town and county…We have heard from a great many refugees who have left Memphis, and have had many words of appreciation for the way they were treated here…I want to thank Mayor Overton and E.H. Crump, Commissioner E.W. Hale, and all governmental agencies of Memphis and Shelby County for the fine way in which they have supported the Red Cross and other agencies.*[226]

The events of 1937 not only mark a turning point in flood control but also illustrate the importance of Memphis regionally and nationally. Memphians played vital roles during and after the superflood by providing the major regional refugee sanctuary and convincing the reluctant federal government to introduce new flood control to the region. Of course other cities played important roles, but a careful examination of sources shows that Memphis was the most influential city in the region during the disaster.

Disasters provide a unique perspective on historical study. They force people from different classes, races and regions to interact in such ways that allow us to observe their world and how they lived at a certain point in time. The suddenness of a disaster generates a great deal of documentation in the press, government records and eyewitness accounts. Such a rich cache of sources covering a short period of time gives us far more information about the character of a population than what one can glean from typical day-to-day accounts. This concentration of overlapping sources provides evidence that defines people's abilities, worldviews and places in society.

The superflood tested the character and resolve of Memphians as they played host to thousands of desperate refugees from the surrounding mid-South while, at the same time, they tried to save their city. Just as the floods stripped away riverbanks, it also exposed some of the inner workings of life in the 1930s. We see how flooding affected the country; how the local political machine worked and the extent of its power; how agencies and communities worked together in times of need; and how mid-southerners interacted. The flood provided insight into the character of Memphians by allowing us to see what roles the city and its citizens played in disaster relief; how local political leaders responded to the flood; and what part Memphians played in flood control.

Memphians, for the most part, followed the Golden Rule, frequently quoted by politicians and preachers of the day. As good Samaritans, they gave what they could to the Red Cross relief fund, organized fundraisers, made donations and volunteered. Memphians risked their lives to rescue stranded flood victims and took in thousands of refugees. The Mayor's Disaster Committee rerouted many arrivals to other facilities during the first days of the flood and, once again, overcrowding became an issue—but Memphians never closed their doors to those in need.

Memphis acted as the region's relief headquarters, primary supply center and shelter to tens of thousands of flood victims from west Tennessee, eastern Arkansas, north Mississippi and southeastern Missouri. The Red Cross and government agencies easily transformed the mid-South's commercial distribution center into a disaster relief supply center. Memphians offered full access to river, rail, air and road transportation services, enabling relief workers to deliver food, medicine and personnel to even the most isolated communities. City officials supplied facilities for housing refugees and supplies, transportation and personnel. Business owners and citizens donated time, materials and money to the Red Cross relief fund. However, Memphians welcomed those escaping the flood but, at the same time, they kept the refugees at a safe distance. Fear of disease and crime led to the mayor's insistence that the flood victims remain behind "a tight military cordon."

We saw events that illustrated the second-class citizenship given to African Americans. While black Memphians had more political influence than other African Americans in the South, the flood shows us that, regardless of inroads made, their civil rights remained tenuous at best. Segregated camps, unequal work and forced labor only proved their low status in society. Even so, African Americans had a sense of community extending beyond the mid-South that allowed them to function outside mainstream white government and media. They raised money and volunteered on behalf of many who may not have received help otherwise.

Ed Crump remained politically secure as his machine emerged from the flood and the subsequent fight for flood-control funding. The flood gave Crump and his lieutenants the opportunity to pursue a comprehensive flood-control plan for Memphis and its passage became viewed as one of the boss's crowning feats. This not only secured the city from future superfloods but it also encouraged companies to remain in Memphis and made the city more attractive to northern business interests.

The events during the flood proved that municipal employees, politicians and average citizens looked to Crump for leadership rather than the mayor or any other elected official. Most importantly, the public saw Crump as a

Epilogue

hero, emphasizing the fact that he was the final authority in Memphis and Shelby County. The boss received numerous letters from businessmen and civic clubs thanking him for saving the city from the flood. In one such letter, L.K. Lawhorn, president of a South Memphis neighborhood association wrote: "The members of the A.B. Hill Co-operative Club wish to extend their sincere thanks and appreciation for the splendid work which you did on the Nonconnah Levee. The people in South Memphis feel that the levee was saved through your efforts alone, and are most grateful."[227]

The machine weathered the storm—but at a price. The organization typically ran smoothly without Crump's constant supervision but the disaster pushed its limits. Crump felt compelled to take charge of the situation after he began to doubt Overton's abilities. Crump's taking the reigns strained the relationship between the boss and the mayor, marking the beginning of an eventual falling out between the two.

Memphians played a part in the battles for greater flood protection in the mid-South. Crump and his supporters—Senator McKellar, Congressman Chandler and others—convinced President Franklin Roosevelt to change his mind to support the inclusion of Memphis in the areas to receive new flood-control measures in 1938. The determination to focus on the tributaries brought an overwhelming scope of new activities throughout the Memphis district of the U.S. Army Corps of Engineers. This meant an abundance of new projects along the Wolf River and Nonconnah Creek and its tributaries and hundreds of new jobs for grateful Depression-era Memphians.[228]

Flood control is not so much a victory over the river as much as it is a temporary cease-fire. No matter what artificial barriers people build or how they try to reroute water, the river will always try to reclaim its territory. Fortunately, the new flood-control measures kept the river at bay each time it tried to reassert itself. The river crested above forty feet at Memphis five more times in the twentieth century but it never again rose as high or caused the amount of devastation, and the city never again had to shelter thousands of refugees or mobilize on such a large scale to rescue flood victims.

Surprisingly, the Ohio–Mississippi Valley Flood of 1937 appears as little more than a footnote in most histories—if even mentioned at all. Many of the events of this tumultuous year soon overshadowed the disaster, leaving it a distant memory in the minds of Americans. In mid-February, a reporter for *Time* magazine wrote, "Crowded out by President Roosevelt's Supreme Court shocker and the fateful automobile strike in Flint and Detroit, the Great Flood of 1937 seeped off the nation's front pages last week." In June, another wrote, "Biggest U.S. news story of 1937 is the resurgence of Labor.

Epilogue

Far longer lived than the Great Flood story and even deeper in its social and political significance than President Roosevelt's battle with the Supreme Court, it is news breaking on a hundred fronts and its ultimate direction and meaning are as exciting as they are as yet unpredictable."[229]

Despite the short memory of most Americans, some Memphians remember the Mississippi River growing into a small sea over three miles wide, swallowing Mud Island and creeping into the low-lying areas of the city. They still remember the thousands of refugees, the sickness and the deaths. They appreciate how charitable Memphians can be—and how cruel. In an interview, a former resident of the Pinch neighborhood in North Memphis, Norris Blackburn, told a reporter that he remembered when sixty thousand cotton bales lined the Pinch's streets east of the river, the campus of Southwestern at Memphis, and at North Parkway and University across from Overton Park. The oblivious reporter asked: "Why?" Blackburn responded: "To keep it dry! That was 1937. Remember there was the big flood in '37."[230]

NOTES

Introduction

1. *Commercial Appeal* (Memphis), "Flooded Families Ask Relief after Attempting Own Aid," February 4, 1937.

The City and the River

2. D.L. Hey and N.S. Philippi, "Flood Reduction through Wetland Restoration: The Upper Mississippi River Basin as a Case History," *Restoration Ecology* 3, no. 1 (1995): 4–17.
3. Zane L. Miller and Patricia M. Melvin, *The Urbanization of Modern America: A Brief History* (New York: Harcourt Brace Jovanovich, 1987), 78.
4. Robert Sigafoos, *Cotton Row to Beale Street: A Business History of Memphis* (Memphis: Memphis State University Press, 1979), 140–145.
5. Sigafoos, *Cotton Row to Beale Street*, 143; Roger Biles, *Memphis in the Great Depression* (Knoxville: University of Tennessee Press, 1986), 18–19.
6. Biles, *Memphis in the Great Depression*, 20–21, 43.
7. John M. Barry, "After the Deluge: As Hurricane Katrina Made Clear, the Lessons of the Mississippi Flood of 1927 (Which Made Herbert Hoover President) Have Yet to be Learned," *Smithsonian* (November 2005): 114–117.

8. Engineering Department, Memphis, TN, *The Memphis Overflow Problem* (Memphis: Paul & Douglas, 1914), 4–5; Report on Flood Control: Memphis, Tennessee, February 1937, Thomas E. Maxson Collection, Memphis–Shelby County Room of the Memphis Public Library and Information Center, series 3, folder 26.
9. Engineering Department, *Memphis Overflow Problem*, 4–5; Barnette Moses, *The Problem of the Mississippi River* (Washington, D.C.: Government Printing Office, 1914), 3–13.
10. Bolton Smith, *Some Mississippi Valley Problems* (Memphis: Southern Alluvial Land Association, 1918), 5–8.

Setting the Stage

11. Barry, "After the Deluge," 114–117.
12. Floyd M. Clay, *A Century on the Mississippi: A History of the Memphis District U.S. Army Corps of Engineers, 1876–1981* (Memphis: U.S. Army Corps of Engineers, 1986), 83.
13. Pete Daniel, *Deep'n As It Come: The 1927 Mississippi River Flood* (Fayetteville: University Of Arkansas Press, 1996), 3–8.
14. Clay, *Century on the Mississippi*, 83.
15. *Memphis Evening Appeal*, "Stage of 42.3 Hits Memphis; Levees Taxed," April 12, 1927; *Memphis Evening Appeal*, "Desert Towns as Dykes Yield to High Water," April 14, 1927.
16. Risk Management Solutions, Inc., *The 1927 Great Mississippi Flood: 80 Year Retrospective* (Newark, CA: Risk Management Solutions, 1997), 4; *Memphis Evening Appeal*, "Issue Warning to Prepare for Huge Overflow," April 15, 1927.
17. U.S. Army Corps of Engineers, Mississippi Valley Division/Mississippi River Commission, *75th Anniversary of the Great Flood of 1927*, March 12, 2002, http://www.mvd.usace.army.mil/offices/pa/releases/2002/Rel0206.pdf (accessed July 27, 2002); "Flood Continued," *Time* 9, no. 20 (May 16, 1927).
18. Gerald M. Capers, *The Mississippi River: Before and After Mark Twain* (Hicksville, NY: Exposition Press, 1977), 77.
19. *Memphis Evening Appeal*, "Red Cross Help for 200,000 is Needed-Hoover," April 25, 1927, 1; *Memphis Evening Appeal*, "Hoover, Here, Gets On the Job Early; Eats Bacon and Eggs," April 25, 1927.

20. *Memphis Evening Appeal*, "Flood Victims from Arkansas Brought Here," April 19, 1927; *Memphis Evening Appeal*, "Refugee Town Here Taking on Normal Aspect," April 23, 1927.
21. *Memphis Evening Appeal*, "Freight Routing Subordinate to Floods-ICC," April 23, 1927.
22. *Memphis Evening Appeal*, "Memphis Heeds Cry for Boats and Provisions," April 23, 1927; *Memphis Press Scimitar*, "Dr. Louis Leroy," May 10, 1944.
23. *Commercial Appeal* (Memphis), "Leroy-Newsum Crew Makes Memphis Port," May 7, 1927.
24. Ibid.
25. "Deluge," *Time* 9, no. 18 (May 2, 1927); "Labors in Rescue Work Made Widows of These Women and Orphans of Children," April 29, 1927.
26. *Commercial Appeal* (Memphis), "Head of Relief Dies in Airplane Crash," May 31, 1927.
27. *Memphis Evening Appeal*, "Vollentine Avenue People Flee Flood," April 15, 1927.
28. Ibid.
29. *Memphis Evening Appeal*, "Fight to Save Memphis Mill Areas Grim," April 16, 1927.
30. *Memphis Evening Appeal*, "Shelby Highways Covered by Floods," April 16, 1927; *Memphis Evening Appeal*, "Bridge Goes Out; Road to South Cut," April 23, 1927.
31. *Memphis Evening Appeal*, "Memphis Prepares for Highest Water," April 18, 1927; *Memphis Evening Appeal*, "Flood Menaces Horn Lake Road: To Stop Travel," April 15, 1927.
32. *Commercial Appeal* (Memphis), "Lightning Hits St. Mary's Cathedral; Organ Damaged," April 21, 1927.
33. *Commercial Appeal* (Memphis), "All Shelby Roads Are Now Open to Travel," April 29, 1927; *Commercial Appeal* (Memphis), "Jefferson Covered with Bayou Waters," May 10, 1927.
34. Kevin R. Kosar, "The Executive Branch's Response to the Flood of 1927," History News Network, October 31, 2005, http://hnn.us/articles/17255.html (accessed November 2, 2009); *Commercial Appeal* (Memphis), "Coolidge Makes Plea for $5,000,000 More to Aid Flood Victims," May, 3 1927.
35. Robert Sigafoos, *Cotton Row to Beale Street*, 140.
36. "On the Coldwater," *Time* 25, no. 5 (February 4, 1935).
37. Clay, *Century on the Mississippi*, 137.
38. Ibid., 138.

Return of the Machine

39. Robert Sharon Allen, *Our Fair City: The Ordeal of Self Government in America* (New York: Vanguard Press, 1947), 232.
40. "Ring-Tail Tooter," *Time* 47, no. 21 (May 27, 1946).
41. Biles, *Memphis in the Great Depression*, 32.
42. Lamar Whitlow Bridges, "Editor Mooney Versus Boss Crump," *West Tennessee Historical Society Papers* 20 (1966): 77–78.
43. David Tucker, "Edward Hull 'Boss' Crump, 1874–1954," *Tennessee Encyclopedia of History and Culture* (Nashville: Tennessee Historical Society, 1998).
44. Charity Organization of the City of New York, "The Common Welfare," *Survey* 28 (April–September 1912): 429–431.
45. Letter from Bride Lee Cawthon to Crump, 2 March 1937, E.H. Crump Collection, Memphis–Shelby County Room, Memphis Public Library & Information Center, 1934, misc. CA-CE, box 142, series 4; Charity Organization of the City of New York, "The Common Welfare," 429–431.
46. Bridges, "Editor Mooney," 87.
47. Capers, *Mississippi River*, 300; David Tucker, "Edward Hull 'Boss' Crump, 1874–1954," *Tennessee Encyclopedia of History and Culture* (Nashville: Tennessee Historical Society, 1998).
48. G. Wayne Dowdy, *Mayor Crump Don't Like It: Machine Politics in Memphis* (Oxford: University Press of Mississippi, 2006), 45–53.
49. Ibid.
50. Sharon D. Wright, *Race, Power, and Political Emergence in Memphis* (New York: Routledge, 1999), 36.
51. Dowdy, *Mayor Crump Don't Like It*, 45–53.
52. Biles, *Memphis in the Great Depression*, 28.
53. Ibid., 34-35.
54. William B. Fowler Papers, 1886–1969, Memphis–Shelby County Room, Memphis Public Library and Information Center, introduction.
55. U.S. Government Printing Office, *Biographical Directory of the United States Congress 1774–2005*, http://www.gpoaccess.gov/serialset/cdocuments/hd108-222/index.html (accessed March 27, 2008); Memphis Mayor Walter Chandler Papers, Memphis–Shelby County Room, Memphis Public Library and Information Center, finding aid.
56. G. Wayne Dowdy, "Expansion of the Crump Machine: Politics in Shelby County, 1928–1936," *West Tennessee Historical Society Papers* 56 (2002), 25.

57. Biles, *Memphis in the Great Depression*, 90.
58. Ibid., 27, 104, 119.
59. Ibid., 90.

January Rain

60. American Red Cross, *The Ohio–Mississippi Valley Flood Disaster of 1937: Report of Relief Operations of The American Red Cross* (Washington, D.C.: American Red Cross, 1938), 17.
61. Bennett Swenson, "Rivers and Floods," *Monthly Weather Review* 65 (February 1937): 72; "Hell and High Water," *Time* 29, no. 5 (February 1, 1937).
62. American Red Cross, *Ohio–Mississippi Valley Flood Disaster*, 10; "Hell and High Water," *Time* 29, no. 5 (February 1, 1937).
63. American Red Cross, *Ohio–Mississippi Valley Flood Disaster*, 11; Grant A. Myer, "Factors Affecting Runoff in *Water: Science and Issue*, ed. E. Julius Dasch, vol. 4 (New York: Macmillan Reference USA, 2003), 64–65; Swenson, "Rivers and Floods," 76.
64. "Hell and High Water," *Time* 29, no. 5 (February 1, 1937).
65. Ibid.
66. "Hell and High Water," *Time* 29, no. 5 (February 1, 1937); *Commercial Appeal* (Memphis), "Red Cross Evacuates Flooded Paducah; Relief Agencies go on 24-Hour Basis to Battle Dangers of Spreading Ohio," January 25, 1937.
67. "Hell and High Water," *Time* 29, no. 5 (February 1, 1937); *Commercial Appeal* (Memphis), "Fear-Crazed Convicts Describe Terrors of Flood Cells," January 26, 1937.
68. "Hell and High Water," *Time* 29, no. 5 (February 1, 1937); *Commercial Appeal* (Memphis), "Fear-Crazed Convicts Describe Terrors of Flood Cells," January 26, 1937.
69. *Commercial Appeal* (Memphis), "Flood Control Fight Turning to Arkansas," January 18, 1937; "Hell and High Water," *Time* 29, no. 5 (February 1, 1937).
70. American Red Cross, *Ohio–Mississippi Valley Flood Disaster*, 14–15; *Commercial Appeal* (Memphis), "55-Foot Crest Predicted for Memphis; Engineer Chief Forecasts 'Super Flood' as Ohio Batters Way into Mississippi," January 26, 1937; *Commercial Appeal* (Memphis), "1200 Families Flee New Pittsburgh Rise," January 26, 1937.

71. *Commercial Appeal* (Memphis), "Crews Work to Save Levees from Threat of Additional Rains," January 17, 1937; "Hell and High Water," *Time* 29, no. 5 (February 1, 1937).
72. "Hell and High Water," *Time* 29, no. 5 (February 1, 1937).
73. "Hell and High Water," *Time* 29, no. 5 (February 1, 1937); *Commercial Appeal* (Memphis), "Levee Tampering Will Mean Death," January 21, 1937.
74. "Hell and High Water," *Time* 29, no. 5 (February 1, 1937); Clay, *Century on the Mississippi*, 146; *Commercial Appeal* (Memphis), "State Orders Troops to Prevent Blasting," January 23, 1937.
75. *Memphis Press Scimitar*, "Slight Earth Tremors Felt at Reelfoot," January 30, 1937; *Commercial Appeal* (Memphis), "Slight Quake is Felt: Temblor in Tiptonville and Reelfoot Lake Area Fails to Cause Damage," January 31, 1937; *New York Times*, "Mississippi Dikes Hold Back Flood: Tiptonville Threat Increases," February 4, 1937.
76. *Commercial Appeal* (Memphis), "Flood Control Fight Turns to Arkansas; Missouri Sees Fall," January 18, 1937; *Commercial Appeal* (Memphis), "Rains Swell Rivers, Boost Flood Danger," January 19, 1937; *Commercial Appeal* (Memphis), "The Swollen Cumberland River Marches on Nashville District," January 22, 1937.
77. "Hell and High Water," *Time* 29, no. 5 (February 1, 1937); *Commercial Appeal* (Memphis), "Mayor Overton Marries Former Bessie Ganong," January 19, 1937.
78. Congressman Walter Chandler of Tennessee, speaking for the funding of flood-control measures in Memphis, on June 15, 1937, 75th Cong., 1st sess., *Congressional Record*: 152612-13987.
79. *Commercial Appeal* (Memphis), "Refugees Directed to Local Red Cross," January 22, 1937; *Commercial Appeal* (Memphis), "Memphis Prepares to Handle 5,000 Refugees If Necessary," January 23, 1937.
80. *Commercial Appeal* (Memphis), "Levees to Hold Burden of Water Rushing South, Army Engineers Believe," January 23, 1937.

High Water Blues

81. Benjamin Albert Botkin, *A Treasury of Mississippi River Folklore: Stories, Ballads, Traditions, and Folkways of the Mid-American River Country* (New York: Crown, 1955), 557.

82. *Commercial Appeal* (Memphis), "Rather Be Dead, Says Refugee in Telling of Flood Terrors," January 25, 1937.
83. *Commercial Appeal* (Memphis), "Flight of Family in Water Waist Deep Told By Mother," January 30, 1937.
84. *Commercial Appeal* (Memphis), "Memphis Prepares to Handle 5,000 Refugees If Necessary," January 23, 1937; E.B. Maynard, *Report on the Sanitary and Health Conditions in Refugee Housing Centers in the City of Memphis*, February 15, 1937, Memphis Mayor Watkins Overton Papers, Memphis–Shelby County Room, Memphis Public Library and Information Center, box 6, series 1.
85. *Commercial Appeal* (Memphis), "Toys, Magazines and Books Are Needed for Refugees," February 3, 1937; *Commercial* Appeal (Memphis), "City Dug in Behind Its Levees and Called Samson's Bluff," January 15, 1967; Maynard, *Report on the Sanitary and Health Conditions*; Kathleen West Caradine, *Works Project Administration, Tennessee Division: 5 District Activities in Mississippi 1937 Flood* (Memphis: Cossitt Library, 1937), 3–7.
86. *Commercial Appeal* (Memphis), "Red Cross Will Set Up Center for Refugees at Fairgrounds," January 24, 1937.
87. Jewish Historical Society of Memphis and the Mid-South, "Julius Lewis: A Philanthropist and a Gentleman," http://www.jhsmem.org/newsletter.htm (accessed March 30, 2010).
88. Maynard, *Report on the Sanitary and Health Conditions*; *Commercial Appeal* (Memphis), "Memphis to Care for 50,000 Refugees; Flood Dead Total 132, Homeless 900,000; Martial Law Rules Two Arkansas Counties," January 27, 1937; *Commercial Appeal* (Memphis), "Flood Crest Estimates Lowered; Army of 100,000 Joins Battle to Strengthen Mississippi Levees," January 29, 1937.
89. *Commercial Appeal* (Memphis), "Refugee Congestion Causes Great Hazard," January 29, 1937.
90. Caradine, *Works Project Administration*, 1–3; Chandler, *Congressional Record*.
91. *Commercial Appeal* (Memphis), "Refugee Congestion Causes Great Hazard," January 29, 1937.
92. Caradine, *Works Project Administration*, 1–3.
93. *Commercial Appeal* (Memphis), "Military Cordon Surrounds 12,000 Refugees in Memphis," January 29, 1937.
94. *Commercial Appeal* (Memphis), "Fairgrounds Fire Quickly Smothered," January 28, 1937.
95. *Commercial Appeal* (Memphis), "Refugees Fight Care," February 1, 1937.

96. *Commercial Appeal* (Memphis), "Flood Victims Urged to Watch for Profiteers," January 30, 1937; *Commercial Appeal* (Memphis), "Four Found Guilty of Red Cross Racket," February 6, 1937; *Commercial Appeal* (Memphis), "Chiselers Reprimanded," February 4, 1937.
97. Chandler, *Congressional Record*; *Chicago Defender*, "LeMoyne College Students Lend a Hand in Memphis Flood Crisis," February 20, 1937.
98. *Chicago Defender*, "LeMoyne College Students Lend a Hand in Memphis Flood Crisis," February 20, 1937.
99. *Commercial Appeal* (Memphis), "Flood Rescue Work Includes Aid for Refugee's Livestock," January 29, 1937; *Commercial Appeal* (Memphis), "Flood Victims Are Warned to Beware of Profiteers," January 30, 1937.
100. *Commercial Appeal* (Memphis), "Flag, Chickens, Broken Churn Among Refugee Possessions," February 1, 1937; Botkin, *Treasury of Mississippi River Folklore*, 546.
101. Botkin, *Treasury of Mississippi River Folklore*, 547.
102. *Commercial Appeal* (Memphis), "Furnished Houses Needed in Memphis," January 29, 1937; *Commercial Appeal* (Memphis), "City Faces Problem in Housing Refugees," January 30, 1937; Maynard, *Report on the Sanitary and Health Conditions*.
103. Maynard, *Report on the Sanitary and Health Conditions*.
104. Letter from E.S. Dudley to Colonel Lawrence Westbrook, March 19, 1937, Dyess, Arkansas, Historical Events, http://www.usacitiesonline.com/ardyessflood1937.htm (accessed 19 January 2010); Michael Streissguth, *Cash: A Biography* (Cambridge: Da Capo Press, 2006), 15.
105. *Forrest City* (Arkansas) *Daily Times-Herald*, "The Facts Justified the Times-Herald Headlines," February 2, 1937.
106. *Commercial Appeal* (Memphis), "1,300 Beds Provided for Ailing Refugees," February 1, 1937; Maynard, "Report on the Sanitary and Health Conditions."
107. *Memphis Press Scimitar*, "Flood Orphans ask Temporary Home," January 30, 1937.
108. *Commercial Appeal* (Memphis), "30,000 Flood Victims Seek Memphis Refuge," February 4, 1937.
109. *Commercial Appeal* (Memphis), "City Centers Battle on Nonconnah Levee," February 2, 1937; Maynard, *Report on the Sanitary and Health Conditions*.
110. *Commercial Appeal* (Memphis), "City Centers Battle on Nonconnah Levee," February 2, 1937; Maynard, *Report on the Sanitary and Health Conditions*.

111. *Commercial Appeal* (Memphis), "City Centers Battle on Nonconnah Levee," February 2, 1937; *Commercial Appeal* (Memphis), "Dr. Lombard Directs Health Forces Here," February 5, 1937.
112. Maynard, *Report on the Sanitary and Health Conditions*.
113. *Commercial Appeal* (Memphis), "Influenza Slows mad Pace of Hollywood Film Capital," January 20, 1937; *Commercial Appeal* (Memphis), "Flu Continues to Spread," January 23, 1937; *Commercial Appeal* (Memphis), Clark Gable Stricken by Attack of Flu," January 23, 1937; Tennessee State Library and Archives, Tennessee Death Certificates for 1937, Microfilm, vol. 1–2.

Flood Capital of the Nation

114. Johnny Cash, *Songs of Johnny Cash*, Amsco Music, 1970.
115. Allen R. Coggins, "Floods of 1937," *Tennessee Encyclopedia of History and Culture* (Nashville: Tennessee Historical Society, 1998); American National Red Cross, *Ohio–Mississippi Flood Disaster*, 116.
116. American Red Cross, *Ohio–Mississippi Valley Flood Disaster*, 45-46.
117. *Commercial Appeal* (Memphis), "For 75 Years Red Cross has Been Alleviating Distress and Suffering-Proves Friend to Mid-Southerners in Time of Disaster and in Daily Life," August 20, 1939.
118. WREC, *Sign-on: The First 50 Years of WREC Radio* (Memphis: WREC, 1972), 34.
119. *Commercial* Appeal (Memphis), "City Dug in Behind Its Levees and Called Samson's Bluff," January 15, 1967.
120. *Commercial Appeal* (Memphis), "Memphians Warned on Fake Solicitors," January 25, 1937.
121. *Commercial Appeal* (Memphis), "Stage Screen Shows Continue to Aid Fund," January 29, 1937; *Commercial Appeal* (Memphis), "Benefit Show Tonight Third in Series Here," January 30, 1937.
122. *Commercial Appeal* (Memphis), "Orpheum will Offer Flood Show Tonight," January 27, 1937; *Commercial Appeal* (Memphis), "Stage Screen Shows Continue to Aid Fund," January 29, 1937; *Commercial Appeal* (Memphis), "Benefit Show Tonight Third in Series Here," January 30, 1937.
123. *New York Times*, "Metlakatla Aids Relief Fund," February 1, 1937; *Commercial Appeal* (Memphis), "Chinese Cable $30,000," February 3, 1937.

124. *Chicago Defender*, "Unfavorable Weather Conditions Force Defender Airplane Down," February 20, 1937; *Chicago Defender*, "Memphis Officially Welcomes Col. John Robinson," March 6, 1937.
125. *Chicago Defender*, "Dan Burley to Tell of Flood At Men's Meet," March 13, 1937.
126. *Commercial Appeal* (Memphis), "Beale Street Show Will Go On Hookup," February 2, 1937; *Commercial Appeal* (Memphis), "Flood News Will Go to British Radios," February 4, 1937.
127. *Commercial Appeal* (Memphis), "WMC Raises Power to Send Warnings," January 24, 1937; WREC, *Sign-on*, 9.
128. WREC, 31.
129. *Commercial Appeal* (Memphis), "Red Cross Shoulders Rescue Work to Free Engineers for Levees," January 27, 1937.
130. *Commercial Appeal* (Memphis), "City Dug in Behind Its Levees and Called Samson's Bluff," January 15, 1967.
131. Caradine, *Works Project Administration*, 8-13; Chandler, *Congressional Record*; *Commercial Appeal* (Memphis), "Engineers Will Buy 60 Outboard Motors," January 24, 1937.
132. *Commercial Appeal* (Memphis), "Memphis Stage at Record High, Officials Ready to Move 20,000 from Backwater Threat in City: Levees Built Higher," January 31, 1937; *Memphis Press Scimitar*, "TVA Comes to Memphis-Lends Aid to Rescue Work," January 30, 1937.
133. *Commercial Appeal* (Memphis), "Colonel Gillette Comes to Memphis," January 29, 1937; *Commercial Appeal* (Memphis), "Air and Boat Fleet Masses for Rescue in Mississippi Area," January 30, 1937.
134. *Commercial Appeal* (Memphis), "Red Cross Shoulders Rescue Work to Free Engineers for Levees," January 27, 1937; *Commercial Appeal* (Memphis), "Air and Boat Fleet Masses for Rescue in Mississippi Area," January 30, 1937.
135. *Commercial Appeal* (Memphis), "Families are Rescued Near Mhoon Landing," February 2, 1937.
136. *Commercial Appeal* (Memphis), "City Dug in Behind Its Levees and Called Samson's Bluff," January 15, 1967.
137. Chandler, *Congressional Record*; *Commercial Appeal* (Memphis), "City Dug in Behind Its Levees and Called Samson's Bluff," January 15, 1967.
138. Chandler, *Congressional Record*; *Commercial Appeal* (Memphis), "Air and Boat Fleet Masses for Rescue in Mississippi Area," January 30, 1937.
139. *Commercial Appeal* (Memphis), "Air and Boat Fleet Masses for Rescue in Mississippi Area," January 30, 1937; *Commercial Appeal* (Memphis), "Blimp Ordered Here," January 29, 1937.

140. *Commercial Appeal* (Memphis), "Pictures Tell the Story of Another Day's Fight in Battle Against River's Flood," February 4, 1937; *Commercial Appeal* (Memphis), "City Faces Problem in Housing Refugees," January 30, 1937.

SUPERFLOOD

141. *Commercial Appeal* (Memphis), "55-Foot Crest Predicted for Memphis; Engineer Chief Forecasts 'Superflood' as Ohio Batters Way into Mississippi," January 26, 1937; *Commercial Appeal* (Memphis), "Reybold Predicts 55-Foot River Stage," January 26, 1937.
142. *Commercial Appeal* (Memphis), "Reybold Predicts 55-Foot River Stage," January 26, 1937.
143. Arlington National Cemetery, "Eugene Reybold, Lieutenant General, United States Army," April 15, 2008, http://www.arlingtoncemetery.net/eugene-reybold.htm (accessed December 17, 2008); U.S. Army Corps of Engineers, "The Benefits of Military Training: Colonel Eugene Reybold and the 1937 Flood," http://www.tpub.com/content/USACEengineeringpamplets2/EP-870-1-45/EP-870-1-450053.htm (accessed December 17, 2008).
144. *Commercial Appeal* (Memphis), "55-Foot Crest Predicted for Memphis; Engineer Chief Forecasts 'Superflood' as Ohio Batters Way into Mississippi," January 26, 1937; *Commercial Appeal* (Memphis), "Reybold Predicts 55-Foot River Stage," January 26, 1937.
145. *Commercial Appeal* (Memphis), "Reybold Predicts 55-Foot River Stage," January 26, 1937.
146. American Red Cross, *Ohio–Mississippi Valley Flood Disaster*, 18; Marion Bragg, *Historic Names and Places on the Lower Mississippi River* (Vicksburg: Mississippi River Commission, 1977; repr., 1990), 4.
147. Clay, *Century on the Mississippi*, 148; *Commercial Appeal* (Memphis), "Engineers to Blast New Madrid Plug with Help of Militia," January 25, 1937.
148. *Commercial Appeal* (Memphis), "Engineers to Blast New Madrid Plug with Help of Militia," January 25, 1937.
149. Clay, *Century on the Mississippi*, 150; *Commercial Appeal* (Memphis), "Refugees Trudge Over Sleet from Bird's Point Floodway," January 28, 1937; *New York Times*, "Scores of WPA Men Fall in Flood Water," February 1, 1937.

150. American Red Cross, *Ohio–Mississippi Valley Flood Disaster*, 19; *Commercial Appeal* (Memphis), "Facts About Valley Flood Listed in Army Bulletin," January 28, 1937; *Commercial Appeal* (Memphis), "Mississippi Valley Ready for Flood Peak," January 31, 1937.
151. *Commercial Appeal* (Memphis), "Hopkins Leads Party Into Memphis Today to View High Waters," February 1, 1937; *Commercial Appeal* (Memphis), "Hopkins Visits Homeless in Camps," February 2, 1937; *Commercial Appeal* (Memphis), "Flood Fighters Check Mississippi; Levees Will Hold Predicted Rise, Engineer Says After Survey," February 2, 1937.
152. *Commercial Appeal* (Memphis), "Flood Fighters Check Mississippi; Levees Will Hold Predicted Rise, Engineer Says After Survey," February 2, 1937.
153. "America's Flood Makes Nearly a Million Refugees," *Life* 2, no. 6 (February 8, 1937), 20–22.
154. *Commercial Appeal* (Memphis), "Flood Fighters Check Mississippi; Levees Will Hold Predicted Rise, Engineer Says After Survey," February 2, 1937.
155. *New York Times*, "Praises Flood Forces," February 6, 1937.
156. *Commercial Appeal* (Memphis), "Rising Flood Waters Leave 500 Families Homeless in South," January 20, 1937; *Commercial Appeal* (Memphis), "River Measures 34.2 Feet on Gauge at Memphis," January 20, 1937; *Commercial Appeal* (Memphis), "Freezing Weather Strikes Memphis with Sleet Storm," January 23, 1937.
157. *Commercial Appeal* (Memphis), "Flood Crest Estimates Lowered; Army of 100,000 Joins Battle to Strengthen Mississippi Levees," January 29, 1937; *Commercial Appeal* (Memphis), "Bureau Will Give Two Gauge Readings in Daily Reports," February 2, 1937.
158. Clay, *Century on the Mississippi*, 147.
159. *Commercial Appeal* (Memphis), "City Sets Machinery Moving to Hold Back Flood Waters," January 17, 1937.
160. *Commercial Appeal* (Memphis), "Rains Cause Closing of Riverside Drive," January 22, 1937; *Commercial Appeal* (Memphis), "Rising Waters Creep on Mid-South Roads," January 23, 1937; *Commercial Appeal* (Memphis), "Rangers Halt Autos on Harahan Viaduct," January 27, 1937; *Commercial Appeal* (Memphis), "Refugees Stream into City as Old Man River Laps Vainly at Memphis' High Bluffs," January 29, 1937.
161. *Commercial Appeal* (Memphis), "Flood Waters Block Mid-South Highways," January 21, 1937.
162. *Commercial Appeal* (Memphis), "Freezing Weather Strikes Memphis with Sleet Storm," January 23, 1937.

163. *Commercial Appeal* (Memphis), "River 3 ¼ Miles Wide at Memphis," February 3, 1937.

164. *Commercial Appeal* (Memphis), "The Mayor's Committee is Ready for Action," February 7, 1937.

165. Gerald M. Capers, *Memphis: Satrapy of a Benevolent Despot* in *Politics and People: The Ordeal of Self-Government in America*, ed. Robert Sharon Allen, rev. ed. (New York: Arno Press, 1974), 212.

Boss Rule

166. Botkin, *Treasury of Mississippi Folklore*, 557.

167. "Crimp in Crump," *Time* 30, no. 18 (November 1, 1937); "The Boss Forgives," *Time* 46, no. 13 (September 24, 1945).

168. Telegram from local businessmen to Crump, 29 January 1937, E.H. Crump Collection Memphis–Shelby County Room, Memphis Public Library and Information Center, misc. FE–FL, box 142, series 4.

169. Dowdy, *Mayor Crump Don't Like It*, 90–91.

170. Flood refugees correspondence, E.H. Crump Collection, Memphis–Shelby County Room, Memphis Public Library and Information Center, folder 3, box 142, series 4.

171. Overton–Crump Correspondence 1937, E.H. Crump Collection Memphis–Shelby County Room, Memphis Public Library and Information Center, folder 3, box 142, series 4.

172. Sigafoos, *Cotton Row to Beale Street*, 186; *Commercial Appeal* (Memphis), "Crump Busy 'Bagging' Wants Permanent Levees in Future," February 3, 1937.

173. *Commercial Appeal* (Memphis), "City Dug in Behind Its Levees and Called Samson's Bluff," January 15, 1967; William B. Fowler Papers, finding aid.

174. *Commercial Appeal* (Memphis), "City Dug in Behind Its Levees and Called Samson's Bluff," January 15, 1967.

175. *Commercial Appeal* (Memphis), "Memphis Stage at Record High; Officials Ready to Move 20,000 from Backwater Threat in City," January 31, 1937; *Commercial Appeal* (Memphis), "City Centers Battle on Nonconnah Levee," February 2, 1937.

176. *Chicago Defender*, "Convicts Freed for Service on Memphis Levee," February 27, 1937.

177. *Memphis Press Scimitar*, "Chain Gang," February 15, 1937.

178. Biles, *Memphis in the Great Depression*, 85; *Commercial Appeal* (Memphis), "City Dug in Behind Its Levees and Called Samson's Bluff," January 15, 1967; Thomas F. Doyle, "Gestapo in Memphis," *Crisis* 44 (May 1941): 152–154.
179. Roy Wilkins, "Through the 1937 Flood Area," *Crisis* 44 (April 1937): 106; *Chicago Defender*, "Dan Burley, Roving Back Door Man Misses Beale Street Blues," February 20, 1937.
180. *Chicago Defender*, "Dan Burley, Roving Back Door Man Misses Beale Street Blues," February 20, 1937.
181. *Chicago Defender*, "Dan Burley, Roving Back Door Man Misses Beale Street Blues," February 20, 1937.
182. Wilkins, "Through the 1937 Flood Area," 124.
183. *Commercial Appeal* (Memphis), "Old Man River Pounds Vainly Against the Doors of South Memphis," February 9, 1937.
184. Senator Kenneth McKellar Papers, General Correspondence, Memphis–Shelby County Room, Memphis Public Library and Information Center, finding aid.
185. Senator Kenneth McKellar Papers, General Correspondence, Memphis–Shelby County Room, Memphis Public Library and Information Center, finding aid; Clay, *Century on the Mississippi*, 154.
186. *Commercial Appeal* (Memphis), "Flood Cost in County Figures at $255,000," February 20, 1937.
187. Chandler, *Congressional Record*.
188. "Hell and High Water," *Time* 29, no. 5 (February 1, 1937).

It's in the Bag

189. "Hell and High Water," *Time* 29, no. 5 (February 1, 1937).
190. Letter from Fowler to Overton, 31 March 1937, Overton Papers, series 1, box 6.
191. *Commercial Appeal* (Memphis), "City Dug in Behind Its Levees and Called Samson's Bluff," January 15, 1967; "Report on Flood Control: Memphis, Tennessee, February 1937" Maxson Collection, series 3, folder 26.
192. Maxson Collection, series 3, folder 26.
193. Ibid.
194. Ibid.

195. Ibid.
196. Ibid.
197. Letter from Overton to McKellar, 19 March 1937, Overton Papers, series 1, box 6.
198. Letter from R.G. Moses to William Fowler, 30 March 1937, letter from Fowler to Overton, 31 March 1937, and copy of letter from William Fowler to Walter Chandler, 31 March 1937, Overton Papers, series 1, box 6.
199. Letter from Chandler to Roosevelt, 20 February 1937, Congressman Chandler, Supreme Court Plan Correspondence and telegram from Chandler to Crump, 15 February 1937, Crump Papers, January 1937–January 1938, box 142, series 4.
200. Telegram from Chandler to Overton, 20 April 1937, Overton Papers, series 1, box 6.
201. Letter from Chandler to Overton, 8 June 1937," Overton Papers, series 1, box 6.
202. 75th Cong., 1st sess., *Congressional Record*, 152612-13987; *Commercial Appeal*, "Flood Plan Lauded Before House," June 16, 1937.
203. Letter from Chandler to Overton, 28 June 1937, Overton Papers, series 1, box 6.
204. Thomas H. Coode, "Kenneth Douglas McKellar, 1869–1957," *Tennessee Encyclopedia of History and Culture* (Nashville: Tennessee Historical Society, 1998).
205. Ibid.
206. Letter from Franklin Roosevelt to McKellar, 30 June 1927, McKellar Papers.
207. Telegram from McKellar to Overton, 10 August 1937; letter from Whittington to Overton, 14 August 1937; and telegram to Chandler to Overton, 14 August 1937, Overton Papers, series 1, box 6.
208. *Commercial Appeal* (Memphis), "Tennessee Had Share in Congress Record," August 22, 1937; *Commercial Appeal* (Memphis), "$13,000,000 Anti-Flood Wall for Memphis is In the Bag," August 29, 1937.
209. Letter from Chandler to Overton, 21 August 1937, Overton Papers, series 1, box 6; *Commercial Appeal* (Memphis), "Mayor Joins Fowler in Rapping Chandler for Project Laxity," August 30, 1937.
210. *Commercial Appeal* (Memphis), "Mayor Joins Fowler in Rapping Chandler for Project Laxity," August 30, 1937; *Commercial Appeal* (Memphis), "City, Chandler Row Awaits Crump Word," August 31, 1937.

211. U.S. Army Corps of Engineers, *Memphis, Wolf River and Nonconnah Creek, Tennessee Flood Control Project* (Memphis: Office of District Engineer, 1950), 1–2; Chandler, *Congressional Record*.
212. "Hell and High Water," *Time* 29, no. 5 (February 1, 1937).

Epilogue

213. John Addington, *A Complete Dictionary of Poetical Quotations* (Philadelphia: J.B. Lippincott and Co., 1855), 57.
214. American Red Cross, *Ohio–Mississippi Valley Flood Disaster*, 21–25.
215. Ibid.
216. Tennessee State Library and Archives, Tennessee Death Certificates for 1937, microfilm, vol. 1–2.
217. *Commercial Appeal* (Memphis), "Mayor's Committee Closes Flood Office," February 16, 1937; *Commercial Appeal* (Memphis), "City Dug in Behind Its Levees and Called Samson's Bluff," January 15, 1937.
218. *Commercial Appeal* (Memphis), "Refugees Started Back to their Homes," February 13, 1937.
219. *Commercial Appeal* (Memphis), "Return of Refugees to Homes, Rehabilitation of the Needy, Red Cross Aim as River Falls," February 18, 1937.
220. Ibid.
221. *Commercial Appeal* (Memphis), "Return of Refugees to Homes, Rehabilitation of the Needy, Red Cross Aim as River Falls," February 18, 1937; *Commercial Appeal* (Memphis), "Mayor's Committee Closes Flood Office," February 16, 1937.
222. *Commercial Appeal* (Memphis), "Coast Guard and TVA Units Leave Memphis," February 18, 1937.
223. Clay, *Century on the Mississippi*, 154.
224. *Memphis Press Scimitar*, "Restore Health of Refugees' Babies," February 16, 1937.
225. *Commercial Appeal* (Memphis), "Mayor's Committee Closes Flood Office," February 16, 1937; *Commercial Appeal* (Memphis), "Memphis Will End Service as Flood Refugee Center," March 15, 1937; *Commercial Appeal* (Memphis), "Clean-up in Shelby Planned," March 14, 1937.
226. *Commercial Appeal* (Memphis), "Memphis Will End Service as Flood Refugee Center," March 15, 1937; *Commercial Appeal* (Memphis), "Clean-up in Shelby Planned," March 14, 1937.

227. Letter from L.K. Lawhorn to Crump, 17 February 1937, Crump Papers, misc. L, box 142, series 4.
228. Clay, *Century on the Mississippi*, 158.
229. "Catastrophe Rolling On," *Time* 29, no. 7 (February 15, 1937); "Press: Newshawks," *Time* 29, no. 26 (June 28, 1937).
230. *Commercial Appeal* (Memphis), "Reunion at Pinch Taps Tales of District," April 22, 1991.

INDEX

A

A.B. Hill Co-operative Club 131
African Americans 16, 24, 25, 26, 27, 37, 38, 40, 54, 60, 63, 64, 66, 67, 72, 77, 80, 106, 108, 109, 130
airplanes 26, 77, 81, 82
Allison, Granville 75
American Car and Foundry 66
American Legion 29, 49, 52, 53, 62
Auction Avenue 27
Austin Powder Company 88

B

Bacon, W.J. 66, 67
Bailey, Carl E. 67
Baker, Henry M. 23, 25, 67
barracks 44, 58, 66, 103
Barron, William E. 23
Bartholomew, Harland 16
Bassett, Arkansas 67

Beale Street/Avenue 64, 94, 106, 108, 109
Belomini, John 37
Benjestown Road 27, 98
Bickford Avenue 27
Big Creek 27
Bird's Point–New Madrid Floodway 46, 87, 88, 89, 110, 126
Birmingham, Alabama 15, 67
Blackburn, Norris 132
Black River 47
Booker T. Washington High School 60, 68
Boy Scouts 62
Braden, Tennessee 66
Breedlove Street 27
Brennan, Joe 76
Brist, Frederick W. 22, 92
British Broadcasting Corporation 77
Browning, F.L. 48
Browning, Gordon 48, 49, 58, 106
Bruce, E.L. Company 16

Index

Buntyn neighborhood 75, 96
Burdick, Roy 87, 88
Burley, Dan 77
Butler, W.O. "Barney" 54, 80

C

Cairo, Illinois 13, 18, 22, 23, 44, 46, 49, 79, 80, 81, 85, 86, 87, 88, 89, 90, 92, 118
Cash, Johnny 67, 73
Central High School 63, 68
Chamber of Commerce 16, 23, 26
Chandler, Albert Benjamin 45
Chandler, Walter 39, 58, 64, 111, 112, 116, 117, 118, 120, 131
Chelsea Avenue 27, 82, 86
Chiang Kai-shek 76
Chickasaw Bluffs 16, 27, 28, 41
Chickasaw Gardens neighborhood 96
children 9, 26, 52, 54, 59, 63, 68, 103, 125, 127
Church, Robert (Bob) Jr. 37, 40, 77
Cincinnati, Ohio 44, 45, 46, 86, 92
circus 54
Civilian Conservation Corps 66, 79, 86
Claridge Hotel 76
Colby, Henry 25
Coldwater River 30, 48
Collierville, Tennessee 67
Colonial Baking Company 53
Commercial Appeal 50, 75, 76, 81, 86, 88, 106
conscription of civilians 106, 109
Coolidge, Calvin 23, 24, 29, 119
Cornelius, W.C. 51, 52
Coyle, Henry 78, 81

criminals 63, 75
Crisis magazine 106, 109
Crump, Edward Hull 24, 33, 34, 35, 36, 37, 38, 39, 40, 41, 49, 50, 100, 101, 102, 103, 104, 106, 109, 111, 112, 113, 116, 120, 129, 130, 131
Cumberland River 22, 23, 46
Cummings School 68
Cypress Creek 82, 94, 98, 115

D

Davis, Clifford 63, 90, 98
Davis, Howard Ellis 79
Delta Highway 28
Denison, S.A. 65, 66
Desoto Fish Dock 64
De Soto, Hernando 13, 14, 65, 66
Dick, Ethel 54
diphtheria 59, 72, 124
Disaster Committee 49, 52, 58, 59, 62, 66, 67, 68, 69, 70, 72, 85, 100, 102, 125, 130
donations for flood relief 24, 75, 76, 130
Doyle, Thomas 106
Driscoll, Dave 77
Dyer County, Tennessee 48, 67
Dyess Colony, Arkansas 67

E

earthquakes 48
Ella Oliver Home 60, 68
Ellet, Charles 18
Ellis Auditorium 51, 52, 58, 59, 63, 64, 69
Ellithorp, Frank A. 23

Index

Estes, Howell M. 69, 70
evacuations 27, 79, 87, 99, 125
Eye, Ear, Nose and Throat Hospital 60

F

Fairgrounds Amusement Park 24, 26, 35, 48, 51, 52, 53, 58, 59, 60, 62, 63, 64, 66, 67, 68, 72, 101, 103, 110, 127
Fairgrounds fire 63
Fairview High School 60, 68, 72, 124
Fayette County, Tennessee 48
Federal Communications Commission 77
Feiser, James L. 23, 89
Fergusson, Harley Bascom 92, 116
Firestone Tire and Rubber Company 41
Fisher Body Works 16
Fletcher, A.H. 70, 126
Fletcher Creek 96
Flood Control Act of 1928 29
Flood control, levees only 16, 18, 29
Flood of 1882 17
Flood of 1912 17
Flood of 1913 17, 27, 89
Flood of 1927. *See* Mississippi Valley Flood of 1927
Floods of 1935 and 1936 30
Ford Assembly Plant 16, 41
Forked Deer River 48
Forrest City, Arkansas 90
Fowler, Toll E. 94
Fowler, William B. 27, 39, 104, 113, 114, 116, 118, 120

G

Ganong, Bessie 49
Gayoso Bayou 16, 17, 27, 83, 93, 104, 114, 115
Gerber, Will 39, 58
Gibson, Walter W. 64
Gillette, Douglass H. 79
Graves, L.M. 59, 70, 126
Grayson, Cary T. 74
Greene, Felix 77
Greenville, Mississippi 23, 25, 26, 28, 80
Griswold, Glenn 112
Gummerie, Richard M. 91

H

Hale, E. William 27, 36, 39, 49, 66, 102, 129
Harahan Bridge 10, 24, 63, 64, 67, 79, 98
Hardwood industry 16
Harrington, Francis C. 89
Hayes, Thomas Henry 77
health department 70, 72, 99, 124, 125
Hindman Ferry Road 27
Hodges Air Field 79
Hoover, Herbert 23, 24, 25, 26, 28, 29, 36, 39, 40
Hopkins, Harry 89, 90, 91, 116
Horn Lake Road 27, 28, 96
Hunt, Bethel T. 66
Hurley, H.G. 79

INDEX

I

influenza 51, 58, 72, 123
Inspector (boat) 90

J

Jackson Avenue 28, 86, 98
Jackson, Sam 49
Jadwin, Edwin 23, 29
Jefferson Avenue 28, 54, 79, 121
Joe Curtis (boat) 80
johnboats 25, 79, 85, 110, 127
Johnson, Roy 93
Jones Avenue 27
Juvenile Court 60

K

Kilpatrick, Earl 26
Knowlton's Point, Arkansas 26

L

Lawler School 60, 68
Leath Bayou 115
Lee, George W. 37, 77, 109
Lee Lumber Company 54
Lee, Tom 25
LeMoyne College 64
Leroy, Louis 25, 79, 80
Lewis, Julius 58
Lick Creek 27, 98, 115
Little Rock, Arkansas 22, 26, 67
Lockhart, Jack 88
Loew Theater 76
Lombard, Marion S. 59, 60, 70
Loosahatchie River 27
Louisville, Kentucky 44, 45, 46, 86, 110

M

Madison Heights neighborhood 98
Madison Heights School 68, 127
Malco Theater 76
Mallory Bayou 115
Marine Hospital 59
Markham, Edward Murphy 89, 90, 91, 92, 113, 116, 117
Marshall, James C. 89
Martin, J.B. 37
Maxson, Thomas E. 104, 114, 115, 116, 121
Maynard, E.B. 69, 70
McKellar, Kenneth Douglas 36, 109, 111, 112, 116, 118, 119, 120, 131
McLain, Tyler 37
Memphis Community Welfare League 77
Memphis Compress and Storage 103
Memphis Flood Control Plan, 1937 116
Memphis, growth of 15
Memphis, image 16, 42, 106
Memphis Municipal Airport 10, 77, 82
Memphis Street Railway 66, 96
Memphis Welfare Committee 49
Metlakatia Indians 76
Mhoon Landing, Mississippi 80
Mississippi River 10, 13, 14, 16, 17, 18, 22, 23, 26, 27, 29, 30, 31, 40, 47, 48, 51, 65, 70, 73, 74, 79, 81, 86, 87, 89, 92, 93, 98, 111, 112, 116, 117, 120, 124, 132
Mississippi River Commission 19

INDEX

Mississippi Valley Flood of 1927 49, 74, 123
Moseley, George Van Horn 69
Moses, Barnette 17
Mud Island 92, 132
mudslides 98
Myer, George 49, 59, 66, 78, 79, 80, 124, 125

N

Nashville, Tennessee 15, 22, 38, 46, 58, 73, 75
National Guard 45, 48, 58, 62, 67, 73, 85, 88, 92
National Youth Administration 59, 62, 86
Navy Yard 28
New Orleans, Louisiana 13, 49, 80, 81, 102
Newsum, Thornton 25
Nonconnah Creek 27, 41, 82, 83, 90, 94, 96, 103, 104, 106, 108, 109, 110, 112, 114, 115, 120, 121, 131
Norman (steamboat) 25
North Memphis 27, 83, 93, 94, 98, 99, 103, 114, 115, 116, 125, 132
North Parkway 94, 132
North Second Street 27, 30, 115

O

Ohio River 22, 30, 44, 45, 46, 81, 83, 114
Omlie, Vernon 26
One Minute Lunch 108
Orange Mound School 60
Orpheum Theater 76
Overall, Joe 80
Overton, Watkins 37, 38, 39, 40, 49, 58, 62, 66, 67, 69, 89, 90, 99, 100, 101, 102, 103, 104, 111, 116, 117, 120, 125, 129, 131, 132

P

Paducah, Kentucky 28, 44, 46, 60, 86
Paine, J. Rowlett 23, 24, 27, 36, 37
Parkin, William 80
Parkview Hotel 76
Parran, Thomas 89
Pauline Street 28
Peabody Hotel 23, 90
Pease, S. Tate 53
Pelican (boat) 26
pneumonia 35, 51, 60, 72, 123
Poinsett County, Arkansas 9
Police Department 24, 35, 37, 94, 108
Prall, A.S. 77
President's Island 39, 80
prisoner labor 27, 46, 62, 104, 106
Public Works Administration 79, 116, 120
pumping stations 17, 27, 93, 115, 121

Q

quarantine 58

INDEX

R

radio 24, 25, 28, 51, 74, 77, 78, 82
railroad 28, 48, 85, 98, 115
Red Cross 10, 21, 23, 24, 25, 26, 28, 44, 46, 49, 51, 52, 53, 54, 58, 59, 62, 63, 64, 66, 67, 69, 70, 73, 74, 75, 76, 78, 80, 81, 85, 89, 92, 102, 103, 104, 110, 123, 124, 125, 127, 129, 130
Reelfoot Lake 48
Reeves, Ray C. 48
Refugees 10, 11, 19, 24, 25, 26, 30, 35, 42, 50, 51, 53, 54, 58, 59, 60, 62, 63, 64, 66, 67, 68, 69, 70, 72, 73, 74, 75, 78, 80, 83, 89, 100, 103, 110, 111, 115, 118, 123, 124, 125, 127, 129, 130, 131, 132
registration of refugees 38, 59, 63
Reid, T. Roy 64
Resolute, blimp 82
Reybold, Eugene 49, 79, 85, 86, 87, 89, 90, 92, 109, 110, 113, 116, 124
Rice, Frank 38, 49
Riverside Drive 30, 94, 96, 98
Robinson, John C. 77
Robinson, Virginia 60
Roosevelt, Franklin Delano 45, 73, 74, 76, 79, 89, 112, 117, 118, 119, 131, 132
Ross, John 49
Rugby Park Road 27

S

sabotage of levees 48
Saffarans Street 93
sanitation 66, 69, 70, 99
Schaefer, Joe 63
Schley, Clinton 49
Searcy, L.J. 77
Sears & Roebuck Company 16
Selmer, Tennessee 66
Shelby County Hospital 60, 68, 72
Shelby County Penal Farm 106
Slavick, Henry W. 77
smallpox 59, 70
Smith, Bolton 18
Southern Alluvial Land Association 18
South Memphis 27, 101, 104, 106, 114, 115, 131
South Memphis Land Company 101, 104
Southwestern College 76, 132
Spalding, George 25
Standard Oil Company 103
Stark, Lloyd C. 47, 88
Sterick Building 75, 127
St. Francis River 9, 23, 30, 47, 50, 93
St. Mary's Cathedral 28
Stone, Mary Lewis 125
streetcars 27
Sunflower Bayou 115

T

Tallahatchie River 30, 48
Tann, Georgia 68
Tech High School 60, 68
Tennessee Children's Home Society 68

Index

Tennessee River 22, 44
Tennessee Valley Authority 79, 126
Terry, W.L. 48
Thain, Doris 125
Thomas Street 94
Tiptonville, Tennessee 48, 79
Tri-State Levee Association 17
Typhoid 24, 45, 59, 70, 72, 124
Tyronza River 52, 67

U

Union Station 45, 64, 75
United States Army Corps of
    Engineers 16, 23, 29, 46, 49,
    79, 85, 89, 102, 131
United States Coast Guard 74, 78,
    81, 126
University of Tennessee 39, 75

V

vaccinations 24, 25, 59
Vogel, Cecil 76
Vollintine Street 27, 98

W

Wabash (boat) 26
Waring, Roane 90
Weaver Road 28
Webb, W.A. 9
West Kentucky Coal Company 98
West Memphis, Arkansas 65, 79,
    90
wetlands 14
WHBQ radio station 77
Whitehaven School 104
White River 30, 47
Whittington, William Madison 89,
    112, 117, 118, 119, 120
Wilkins, Roy 109
Williams, Oscar P. 39, 83
WMC radio station 24, 25, 51, 77,
    87
WNBR radio station 77
Wolf River 27, 30, 41, 48, 82, 83,
    86, 94, 96, 114, 116, 120,
    125, 131
Women's Professional Projects 60
Works Progress Administration 53,
    54, 60, 62, 86, 89, 96, 104,
    106, 126
WREC radio station 75, 77, 87

ABOUT THE AUTHOR

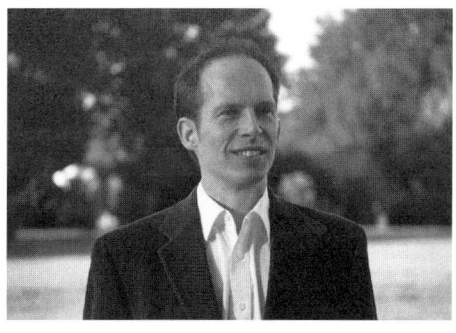

Patrick W. O'Daniel is a professional librarian in Memphis, Tennessee. He worked for the Memphis Public Library & Information Center for over sixteen years, spending nine years in the History–Social Sciences Department working with archival and genealogical collections. He has a Master's Degree in history from the University of Memphis, a Master's Degree in information sciences from the University of Tennessee, Knoxville, and he has studied at the Institute of Genealogy and Historical Research at Samford University in Birmingham, Alabama. Patrick lives in Memphis with his wife, Kathy, and daughter Kelly.

Visit us at
www.historypress.net